FREE AND CLEAR

FREE AND CLEAR

GOD'S ROADMAP TO DEBT-FREE LIVING

HOWARD DAYTON

MOODY PUBLISHERS

CHICAGO

The name Crown Money Map™ is a trademark of Crown Financial Ministries.

All Scripture quotations, unless otherwise indicated, are taken from the *Holy Bible, New International Version®*. NIV®. Copyright © 1973, 1978, 1984 by International Bible Society. Used by permission of Zondervan Publishing House. All rights reserved.

Scripture quotations marked NASB are taken from the *New American Standard Bible®*, Copyright © 1960, 1962, 1963, 1968, 1971, 1972, 1973, 1975, 1977, 1995 by The Lockman Foundation. Used by permission.

Scripture quotations marked TLB are taken from *The Living Bible*, copyright © 1971. Used by permission of Tyndale House Publishers, Inc., Wheaton, Illinois 60189. All rights reserved.

Scripture quotations marked NLT are taken from the *Holy Bible, New Living Translation*, copyright © 1996. Used by permission of Tyndale House Publishers, Inc., Wheaton Illinois 60189. All rights reserved.

Scripture quotations marked NKJV are taken from the *New King James Version*. Copyright © 1982 by Thomas Nelson, Inc. Used by permission. All rights reserved.

Scripture quotations marked AMP are taken from *The Amplified Bible*. Copyright © 1965, 1987 by The Zondervan Corporation. *The Amplified New Testament* copyright © 1958, 1987 by The Lockman Foundation. Used by permission.

Cover Designer: The DesignWorks Group
Cover Image: Corbis
Interior Designer: Smartt Guys Design
Editor: Jim Vincent

Library of Congress Cataloging-in-Publication Data

Dayton, Howard Lape, 1943-
    Free and clear : God's roadmap to debt-free living / Howard Dayton.
        p. cm.
    Includes bibliographical references (p.   ).
    ISBN-13: 978-0-8024-2257-6
    1. Finance, Personal—Religious aspects. 2. Money—Religious aspects. 3. Debt. I. Title.

HG179.D368 2006
261.8'5—dc22

                                                                          2005034714

We hope you enjoy this book from Moody Publishers. Our goal is to provide high-quality, thought-provoking books and products that connect truth to your real needs and challenges. For more information on other books and products written and produced from a biblical perspective, go to www.moodypublishers.com or write to:

Moody Publishers
820 N. LaSalle Boulevard
Chicago, IL 60610

ISBN: 0-8024-2257-8
ISBN-13: 978-0-8024-2257-6

3 5 7 9 10 8 6 4 2

Printed in the United States of America

Dedicated to Larry Burkett (1939–2003),
cofounder of Crown Financial Ministries.
A close friend and godly man,
who was used by the Lord in an extraordinary way.

Contents

Acknowledgments

want to express my deepest gratitude to Steve Gardner, Mark Tobey, and Greg Thornton for helping to make this book a reality. And to my awesome wife, Bev Dayton, I appreciate your relentless encouragement.

This book would not have been possible without the Crown Financial Ministries leadership team of Dave Rae, Stan Reiff, Chuck Bentley, Dr. Dick Wynn, Bob Yarbrough, Rob Parker, and James Massa.

And to all those who serve with Crown, thank you for your commitment to help people get out of debt so that they may enjoy *True Financial Freedom*.

God's roadmap is the only reliable guide to lead you, no matter your situation, to experience the joy and blessing of true financial freedom—free and clear from the stress and strain of debt.

CHAPTER ONE

The **Problem**

Tim Connor slammed the front door behind himself in disgust. He and his wife, Cindy, had been arguing about money—*again*. As their burden of debt had grown, so had the frequency and intensity of their conflicts. He had to get out of the house to clear his mind.

Tim couldn't believe what he had said to Cindy in his anger: "Your middle name is spending! You waste money more than anyone I know! And I'm the one going to work every day!"

Cindy had shot back, "At least I didn't buy a new bass boat using a credit card! How stupid was that! And you think I waste money. Give me a break! I'm so tired of fighting about this stuff. I don't think I can take this too much longer, Tim. This just isn't working. Maybe we should get a divorce."

"What are you saying?" Tim yelled back. "You really want to leave me, don't you?" With that, Cindy had started to cry. She retreated in tears to their bedroom, angry, frustrated, and feeling alone.

Tim's heart filled instantly with regret. He couldn't believe it had come to this. *Was she really suggesting divorce?* Tim thought of their two young children and how much they loved their mother. He loved her too. He had always considered their marriage—nine years long at this point—a success. From the outside, everything looked picture perfect. Yet, somehow this latest blowup was different from the past squabbles he and Cindy had had over money. He had seen desperation in her eyes that he had not seen before. And now that the "D" word had surfaced, it was clear the debt pressure had begun to turn their financial disagreements into a potential marriage breaker.

The truth is Tim and Cindy's financial stress did not develop overnight. This was no sudden turn for the worse. What they were experiencing is all too common in this buy-now-pay-later culture in which we live. In fact, in most situations I've been involved with in helping people get out of debt, their troubles had developed and intensified almost imperceptibly—like a storm gathering on a horizon.

A GATHERING STORM

In the last fifty years meteorologists have discovered the secrets of how hurricanes develop. A monster Category 5 hurricane that unleashes its catastrophic destruction when it makes landfall in the eastern United States can begin with a gentle weather pattern of warm air rising in the plains of western Africa. Soon a growing thunderstorm moves out over the tropical Atlantic Ocean waters, and then, in stages, becomes a tropical depression, a tropical storm, and finally a full-blown hurricane. Hurricanes start small and gain in intensity—just like problems and conflicts over debt.

That's precisely what happened with Tim and Cindy. They allowed the problem to go too long before they addressed it honestly.

Though they had overcome earlier challenges that grew out of their different family backgrounds, they never thought that their financial problems brought on by worry over debt would soon threaten everything.

Cindy had been raised in a middle-income family and, as the apple of her father's eye, got anything she wanted. She learned to expect a life of relative ease and comfort that caused her to take hard work and sacrifice for granted. Tim, in contrast, knew firsthand the struggles of tight finances. He had grown up on a farm, the third of five children. With never enough money to go around, his parents had seemed to be in a never-ending squabble about how they were going to make ends meet. Often he could hear his mother cry herself to sleep. Even as a youngster, Tim had gone to bed imagining that his family might be out on the street the next day.

FREE AND CLEAR: THE ROAD TO FREEDOM

For some reason, Tim and Cindy had never really discussed with each other their hopes and dreams—or their fears—regarding their future. They had never talked about how they wanted to use money to fulfill those dreams. They, like many other people, had unspoken expectations they didn't fully understand. They are not alone, and neither are you.

God loves you and cares deeply about you. He knew that money would be a challenge for us and wanted to help us manage it wisely. That's why He said so much about it. You may be surprised to know that the Bible contains 2,350 practical verses on how to handle money and possessions. Indeed, 15 percent of everything Jesus Christ said in the Scriptures dealt with money and possessions!

In this book you will learn God's way to get out of debt.

God's roadmap is the only reliable guide to lead you, no

matter your situation, to experience the joy and blessing of true financial freedom—free and clear from the stress and strain of debt.

TAKING STOCK

This section at the end of each chapter will help you to measure your progress as you follow God's roadmap toward becoming free and clear of debt.

1. Circle the word below that best describes your current financial situation (If you're married, see if you and your spouse chose the same word. Then discuss your responses.)

Manageable   *Challenging*   *Stressful*   *Desperate*

2. What do you believe is your greatest barrier to getting out of debt?

We've all made mistakes with money in the past.

Do not let a sense of guilt overwhelm you;

rather, learn from the experience.

CHAPTER TWO

The **Answer**

Cindy and Tim Connor called to ask for help on Crown's nationally broadcast radio program, *Money Matters*. At the time they called they were desperate. "We're under a mountain of debt and headed for a breakdown in our marriage," Tim admitted. "So we have to get out of it—no matter what it takes."

I was about to ask Cindy if she agreed with Tim, but before I had a chance, she added, "We really need help. We know we have to do this, but we're not sure where to start."

I sensed in their voices that they were a very determined couple. They lived close to the offices of Crown Financial Ministries, so I invited them to meet with me to examine their financial situation.

We met a week later. Tim was quite nervous. He was teaching music at a high school and tutoring students on the side to earn additional income. Cindy worked two days a week as a nurse at the local hospital. They also had two small children, both starting school. Tim and Cindy looked stressed. Tim stammered, "I'm not sure if we just don't make enough money or if we're spending too much." Cindy added, "One thing is for sure; we don't understand where it's all going."

A GROWING DILEMMA

The Connors faced an all-too-common dilemma: They had gotten way over their heads in debt. They didn't really know the extent of the problem. What they needed to do first was take an honest look at their situation.

The Connors owed a substantial amount to retail stores, doctors, credit card companies, and their bank. Tim, remember, had just bought a shiny new fishing boat—using plastic! In addition, they carried a sizeable home mortgage. Their growing family meant increasing expenses, and in a few years they would need college tuition for the children. Neither Tim nor Cindy could foresee a brighter future. They felt stuck.

Because of their debts, the Connors tried to shop carefully, sometimes comparing half a dozen outlets for the best price. Tim determined to handle most of the car maintenance, and Cindy avoided buying expensive convenience foods. But the family faced a critical problem. They never had been able to plan their spending. They seldom decided not to buy what they wanted, and they had no plan to save or invest for the future. They had fallen into the debt trap.

THE DEBT EXPLOSION

Unfortunately, the Connors join millions of Americans struggling under the weight of personal debt. Government, business, and personal debt continue to explode in our country. Each day, our mailboxes are flooded with tantalizing credit card offers promising an introductory low percentage rate for the first few months. For many cash-strapped individuals, that's an offer too good to refuse! We have so much debt that the average person has been described as someone driving on a bond-financed highway in a bank-financed car fueled by credit-card-financed gas, going to purchase furniture on the installment plan to put in his mortgaged home! Sound familiar?

Forty-three percent of all families spend more than they earn each year. In fact, most of them spend about 10 percent more than they earn: That's $1.10 spent for every dollar earned. How long can that continue? Before long they're in financial bondage.

Look at the incredibly rapid increase in debt reflected in these graphs.

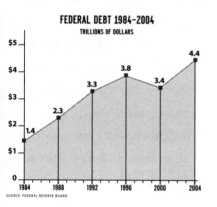

FEDERAL DEBT 1984–2004
TRILLIONS OF DOLLARS

SOURCE: FEDERAL RESERVE BOARD

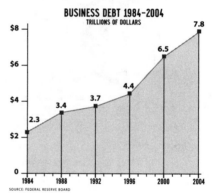

BUSINESS DEBT 1984–2004
TRILLIONS OF DOLLARS

SOURCE: FEDERAL RESERVE BOARD

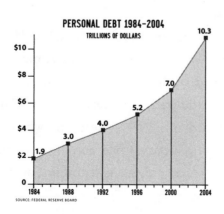

PERSONAL DEBT 1984–2004
TRILLIONS OF DOLLARS

SOURCE: FEDERAL RESERVE BOARD

With that kind of out-of-control spending and mounting debt, it's no wonder so many people suffer from debilitating stress.

THE REAL COST OF DEBT

Debt damages more than our personal finances; it also often increases stress, which contributes to mental, physical, and emotional fatigue.

" TILL DEBT DO US PART"

© Marc Shaw. Used by permission.

It can compromise health and, at times, lead to serious illness. It can harm relationships and marriages. According to surveys, tension in the home over money is one of the most common causes of divorce.

Many people raise their lifestyle by using debt, only to discover that the burden of debt then controls their lifestyle. Before they know it they're drowning in debt and desperate for a rescue plan.

BEEN THERE, DONE THAT

When the Connors shared their predicament, I understood completely. Sometimes when I give a talk to people about money, I begin by saying, "Hi, I'm Howard Dayton, and I'm a recovering addict." Early in my marriage I was addicted to material things! Gaining more and more stuff consumed my life to the point where before learning God's way of handling money, I had gotten us in tens of thousands of dollars in debt. We had only a small amount of savings, and I gave little.

However, once I learned and applied God's financial principles, everything changed. And I mean everything! It didn't happen overnight, but within nine years, my wife, Bev, and I were debt-free—free and clear of everything, including our home. We went from financial bondage, and all the stress and strain that brings, to true financial freedom. Words cannot describe how good we felt. And now, I want you to experience that same freedom.

Someone once told me that the Lord often allows a person to teach a subject because the teacher desperately needs it! That was certainly true for me in the area of money. I have never met anyone who had more wrong attitudes about money or who handled money in a way more contrary to the Bible than I did.

Some who read this book are deeply in debt. Others are on the road to trouble and don't yet realize it. But if you're like Tim and Cindy, stuck in financial bondage, there is hope. You can become debt-free! You can do it!

By the way, we've all made mistakes with money in the past. Do not let a sense of guilt overwhelm you; rather, learn from the experience. The apostle Paul said it this way: *"Forgetting what lies behind and reaching forward to what lies ahead, I press on toward the goal"* (Philippians 3:13–14 NASB). It's time to stop focusing on the problem and turn to the solution.

THE ANSWER

Increasingly, people wonder where they can turn for financial advice and for real solutions to their financial problems. There are two basic choices: the Bible and the answers people devise. The way most people handle money is in sharp contrast to God's financial principles. Isaiah 55:8 reads, "'For my thoughts are not your thoughts, neither are your ways my ways,' declares the LORD."

The purpose of this book is to help you learn what God says about debt and then to provide you simple, proven steps to get out of it. It offers practical ways to integrate these biblical principles into your life. As you discover these principles and put them into practice, you will begin to enjoy profound spiritual freedom. And you'll be on the road to experiencing true financial freedom.

So if you're looking for the answers to your debt dilemma, you've found it. The answers are found in the timeless pages of the Bible.

Remember: The principles you will be learning are a gift from a loving heavenly Father—a gift intended to benefit you.

Are you ready? Good. Let's hit the road to true financial freedom.

TAKING STOCK

1. If God's ways are not our ways, how do we discover what He thinks about money?

2. Why do you think most people have such faulty views of debt and how to handle money?

3. One of the Bible verses quoted in this chapter came from the book of Philippians. Remember it? *"Forgetting what lies behind and reaching forward to what lies ahead, I press on toward the goal."* List some of the attitudes and mistakes regarding your handling of money you'd like to leave behind.

4. Finally, list three of the most important goals you wish to achieve financially.

-

-

-

There is a division of responsibilities in the handling of our money. God has certain responsibilities, and He has given other responsibilities to us.

CHAPTER THREE

A God's-Eye View of Money

A t the end of my initial meeting with the Connors, I told them, "Your first step in getting out of debt is to learn what God says about money."

It's the first step for anyone. And you may be just like Tim, who sheepishly admitted he had no idea the Bible had so much to say about money. I certainly could relate to that.

WHERE IT ALL BEGAN

Several years ago, I was just as surprised to discover how much the Bible had to say about money. My business partner, Jim Seneff, and I found ourselves making financial decisions for our expanding business and young families without any scriptural point of reference. I desired, along with Jim, to be the best husband and the best business-man I could be. We both wanted to follow God's roadmap to a life of financial freedom. In order to do that we decided to do a thorough study of what Scriptures said about money. Together we read the entire Bible, locating each of the 2,350 verses that dealt with money and possessions, and arranged those verses by topics.

The results were dramatic. What emerged from that study were powerful principles for the use of money and possessions—principles that literally changed our lives.

In addition to putting those principles into practice in our own families and business, we put what we had discovered into a seminar and presented it at our church. We witnessed a remarkable response! People bombarded us with questions, describing areas of intense frustration.

Later I founded Crown Ministries, which merged with Larry Burkett's Christian Financial Concepts to form Crown Financial Ministries. Crown has developed practical materials to help people of all ages get on the road to true financial freedom. Tens of thousands of churches around the world now use Crown's material to teach people biblical financial principles. We're convinced the material has been so effective because God's plan is the only plan for true financial freedom.

AN OVERVIEW OF GOD'S PERSPECTIVE

Because it's so important to understand God's way of handling money, let me give you a brief overview. I'm convinced Jesus said so much about money for two reasons:

1. How we handle our money impacts our fellowship with Him.
2. He wants to help us handle money wisely.

Money Matters and Our Fellowship

How we handle our money impacts our fellowship with Christ. Jesus revealed a direct relationship between how we handle our money and the quality of our spiritual lives. In Luke 16:11, He asks a penetrating question: "So if you have not been trustworthy in handling worldly wealth, who will trust you with true riches?" You can't get any clearer than that!

I discovered that every time I applied one of God's financial principles, I found myself drawn closer to Christ. However, if I was unfaithful with even one, my fellowship with Him suffered. But there's another reason why Jesus taught so specifically on the handling of money.

Money Matters and God's Roadmap

God wants to help us handle money wisely. He realizes that money plays a big part in our lives. We spend much of our time working for it, deciding how to spend it, grappling with debt, thinking about where to save and invest, and praying about giving. The Lord knew money would be a challenge, even a source of conflict for many of us.

He wants to help us handle money wisely, so He has given us clear, practical truths in the Bible that really work. They are His roadmap to guide us on our financial journey.

WHERE THE BUCK REALLY STOPS

There is a division of responsibilities in the handling of our money. Simply put: God has certain responsibilities, and He has given other responsibilities to us. Most frustration in handling money comes because we do not realize which responsibilities are ours and which belong to the Lord. It will be helpful for you to understand this division as you evaluate your current situation.

God's Responsibility—the Owner

God created all things and owns everything. God's primary responsibility in relation to money and possessions is to act as the owner. Psalm 24:1 tells us, *"The earth is the LORD's, and everything in it."* Scripture gets even more specific. Leviticus 25:23 identifies God as the owner of all the land: *"The land must not be sold permanently, because the land is mine and you are . . . my tenants."* Haggai 2:8 says He owns all the mineral riches of the earth: *"'The silver is Mine and the gold is Mine,' declares the LORD Almighty."*

When we acknowledge God's ownership, our perspective on money and possessions changes. Every spending decision becomes a spiritual decision. No longer do we ask, "Lord, what do You want me to do with *my* money?" The question becomes, "Lord, what do You want me to do with *Your* money?" When we have this attitude and handle His money according to His wishes, spending decisions are just as spiritual as giving decisions.

Our Responsibility—the Stewards

The word that best describes our responsibility is *steward*. Stewards manage someone else's possessions or money. Our responsibility is summed up in this verse: *"It is required in stewards that one be found faithful"* (1 Corinthians 4:2 NKJV).

Before we can be found faithful, we must know what we are required to do. Just as the operator of a complicated piece of machinery studies the manufacturer's manual to learn how to operate it, we need to examine the Owner's manual—the Bible—to determine how He wants us to handle His possessions.

The 100 Percent Rule for Stewards

As stewards of *His* possessions, God wants us to be faithful in handling *all* of our money. Unfortunately, most Christians have been taught how to handle only 10 percent of their income God's way—the area of giving. And although this area is crucial, most have relied on the world's wisdom to learn how to handle the other 90 percent. No wonder so many Christians are struggling under the weight of bad financial decisions. God's plan is for us to handle 100 percent of our finances and possessions His way.

Thankfully, the Bible tells us how to earn, spend, give, save, invest, get out of debt, and teach our children how to handle money. In short, everything we need to know about handling money wisely is found in the Bible.

CORRECTING YOUR COURSE

Since most Christians have not been equipped to handle money biblically, many of them develop wrong attitudes. That results in disastrous financial decisions and the painfully unnecessary consequences that follow. Tim and Cindy Connor are perfect examples. They faced what seemed to them an impossible road ahead. God said in Hosea 4:6 that *"my people are destroyed from lack of knowledge."* Once people begin looking closely at God's way of handling money, many discover areas in which they have not been faithful. You may be one of those people. If so, don't be discouraged. The Lord is kind and merciful, and He wants the best for you. God wants to help you correct your course.

As we apply God's principles to our finances, we will begin to get out of debt, spend more wisely, start saving for our future, and give even more to the work of Christ. But the first step in getting out of debt God's way is learning how God feels about it. So let's again turn to the pages of the Bible to find out God's perspective.

WHAT THE BIBLE SAYS ABOUT DEBT

God's perspective on debt is clear. Look closely at the first portion of Romans 13:8 from several different Bible translations: *"Let no debt remain outstanding"* (NIV). *"Pay all your debts"* (TLB, NLT). *"Owe nothing to anyone"* (NASB). *"Keep out of debt and owe no man anything"* (AMP). Are there any questions about what the Lord wants for us concerning debt? Likely not at this point. The Bible makes it abundantly clear. God's will for you is to be free and clear of debt.

Avoid Bondage

In Proverbs 22:7, we learn the primary reason why God speaks so strongly against debt: *"The borrower is servant to the lender."* When you go in debt, you place yourself in bondage to the lender. The deeper in debt you go, the stronger the bondage. You quickly forfeit the freedom to decide where to spend your income; you legally obligate yourself to repay your debts.

Slavery to debt is not what your heavenly Father wants for you. He wants His children to be free and clear from the bondage and stress associated with debt.

The Lord discourages debt for two additional reasons.

Avoid the Curse of Debt

First, freedom from debt is a reward. Debt is a curse.

In the Old Testament, God promised freedom from debt as a reward for obedience. *"If you fully obey the LORD your God and carefully follow all his commands I give you today, the LORD your God will set you high above all the nations on earth. All these blessings will come upon you. . . . You will lend to many nations but will borrow from none"* (Deuteronomy 28:1–2, 12b). God promised to bless His people with a freedom from debt if they were obedient to Him.

However, the Lord warned the people of Israel of the curse of debt for disobedience. Later in Deuteronomy 28, God declared:

If you do not obey the LORD your God and do not carefully follow all his commands and decrees I am giving you today, all these curses will come upon you and overtake you. . . . The alien who lives among you will rise above you higher and higher, but you will sink lower and lower. He will lend to you, but you will not lend to him. He will be the head, but you will be the tail." (Deuteronomy 28:15, 43–44)

When we willfully disobey God's clear principles of finance, we cannot expect His blessing on our finances.

Recognize That the Future Is Uncertain

Second, debt presumes upon the future.

When you get into debt, you assume you'll earn enough in the future to repay your debts along with interest. You plan for your job to continue or your business or investments to be profitable. But the Bible cautions against such presumption:

Now listen, you who say, "Today or tomorrow we will go to this or that city, spend a year there, carry on business and make money." Why, you do not even know what will happen tomorrow. What is your life? You are a mist that appears for a little while and then vanishes. Instead, you ought to say, "If it is the Lord's will, we will live and do this or that." (James 4:13–15)

ASK THE LORD

Now, you may be thinking you're too far in debt to ever recover. That's simply not true. No matter your situation, God wants you to be free, and He has provided a roadmap for you to follow. All you need to do is take the first step toward freedom: Turn to the Lord for help.

In 2 Kings 4:1–7 we read about a widow who faced losing her children as slaves to her creditor. How times have changed! The desperate mother appealed to the prophet Elisha for help.

Elisha instructed the woman to borrow empty jars from her neighbors. Once she had gathered all the jars in her home, she shut the door behind her as the prophet instructed her to do. Then the Bible tells us that the Lord supernaturally multiplied her only possession—a small amount of oil—filling all the jars. She sold the oil and paid her debts to free her children.

The widow had asked God for help, and God answered her prayers.

The same God who provided supernaturally for the widow will help you become free and clear of debt too. The first and most important step is to pray. Seek the Lord's help and guidance in your journey toward D-Day—your Debtless Day. God may act immediately or gradually, over time. Leave that to Him. In either case, your prayerful trust in Him and His involvement in your finances are essential.

I see good things happening to God's people when they trust God's plan for their finances. In fact, I see a trend emerging: As people begin to eliminate debt, the Lord is blessing their faithfulness. He can multiply *your* efforts as well.

TAKING STOCK

1. How would you assess your willingness to follow God's principles for handling money? Circle one.

   Still not ready   *Ready but unsure*   *Ready and willing*

2. What encouragement can you draw from understanding that God is the owner and you are the steward, or manager?

3. How do you feel about being a servant to a lender?

Prayer to Go Forward:
Dear Lord, I'm ready to follow Your financial plan. Forgive me for any past mistakes I've made. Help me do what's best from this point forward. Amen.

The Money Map is a proven, step-by-step guide that works for *everyone* regardless of their financial situation.

CHAPTER FOUR

The **Money Map**

I invited the Connors to have dinner with Bev and me at our home.

Over the meal, Tim and Cindy shared that for the first time in a long time they had financial hope. They realized the decision to become debt-free was one of the most important of their married life, and they could feel their relationship improving. The stress and hopelessness of financial bondage were giving way to their newfound vision for freedom.

Tim recognized that Cindy had a need for financial stability, that she felt more secure in their marriage when their finances were in good shape. Cindy agreed, noting, "Instead of spending and complaining, I'm starting to think of ways to cut expenses."

"We're finding it easier to discuss our finances without fighting," Tim added. "The only missing piece seems to be a clear picture of what to do next. We just don't know."

"That's one of the reasons we asked you to come tonight,"

Bev said while bringing out the dessert. "After we finish dinner, Howard wants to take a few minutes to show you Crown's Money Map. I think you'll love how clear and simple it makes everything. It's the same journey Howard and I have taken to become financially free, except now you don't have to figure it out for yourself. I wish it had been around when we were your age."

After dinner, we spread a copy of Crown's Money Map on the table. Tim glanced at the graphics and clearly marked destinations—all appearing in logical order—and said, "This is what we've been looking for!"

It's the journey Bev and I have been on for thirty years. When Bev and I started our journey, we were in the same place financially that Tim and Cindy were in: frustrated and trapped in financial bondage. But the Lord gave us the desire to work toward true financial freedom—to get in a position where we didn't need to earn a salary to meet our needs. We wanted to be able to volunteer our time to serve our church or a ministry without having to receive a wage.

We knew this would take a *long* time and require a lot of effort, but that by God's grace it was possible. We also understood that "a trip of a thousand miles begins with one step." We needed a plan with small, achievable steps along the way. We lived what eventually developed into the Crown Money Map™, and for the past twenty years I have been privileged to serve as a full-time volunteer at Crown. That's why I'm so excited about sharing the Crown Money Map with you.

THE MONEY MAP

We have developed the map to help people on their journey to true financial freedom. It is a proven, step-by-step guide that works for *everyone* regardless of their financial situation. Some people may not reach the final destination, but everyone can make progress, and each destination along the way brings greater financial freedom.

The map is easy to understand and follow. You can record your progress on the map or use the supporting Web site. To see the interactive version and order your copy, go to www.crownfreeandclear.org. Crown also offers live, free, online Money Map coaching to help you. And as I said, every major goal worth pursuing begins with a first step.

WHAT'S YOUR PURPOSE IN LIFE?

Big Rocks First

This may surprise you, but we have learned that before you start your journey, the first step is to identify your life purpose and set short-term and long-term goals.

A teacher brought a large glass jar to class. She filled it with big rocks and asked the class, "Do you think the jar is full?"

"Yes," the students immediately responded.

Then, she reached under her desk and brought out a bag of small pebbles that she poured into the jar. Again she asked, "Now, do you think the jar is full?"

This time the class hesitated. Several of the students finally said, "I think so."

Once again, she pulled out a bag, this time containing sand. She shook the jar as she emptied the bag of sand. "Now, I want you to think carefully. Do you think the jar is now full?" the teacher asked.

The class was silent. One last time she reached down and brought out a pitcher of water and filled the jar to the brim.

"Now," she said, "the jar is full. Here's what I want you to remember from this demonstration. You have to put in the big rocks first. If you fill the jar with the other things, you won't have room for the big rocks.

"Imagine that your life is this jar. And the most important things in your life are represented by the big rocks. Make sure you do the important things before you fill your life with the less important."

The Biggest Rock: Your Purpose in Life

I'm convinced that of all the "big rocks" on your financial journey, the biggest is your life purpose—the vision for your life. That's why it's important at this stage to take time to be quiet before the Lord, asking Him to clarify the really important things He wants you to do. This process will help answer the big questions, such as:

- What three things do I want to accomplish during my lifetime?
- If my life turned out well, what would it look like?
- For what do I want to be remembered?

If you are married, answer these questions individually and then take some time to pray and discuss your answers with each other. Decide on a life purpose for your marriage.

For example, my life purpose is: (1) To influence my family and friends to know Jesus Christ as their Savior and to grow close to Him, (2) To teach as many people as possible God's financial principles, and (3) To leave the legacy of practical financial materials based on the Bible.

Setting Goals to Reach Your Life Purpose

Once you have identified your life purpose, establish short-term and long-term goals. These are achievable steps that will help you reach your life purpose. For instance, if you are a working mother of young children and you want to stay home to raise them, consider the steps you will need to take. These become your goals. You will need to make ends meet on just your husband's income. Goals might include paying off certain debts, perhaps selling a vehicle, or even moving to more affordable housing.

Writing your goals is a powerful but often neglected step that helps you clarify and prioritize them. The mystery fades as you monitor your progress and make midcourse corrections. Written goals create momentum, helping you focus on the priorities that will achieve your life purpose.

Bev and I came to understand that money was simply a tool—one that helps us accomplish the goals we needed to achieve to reach our life purpose.

HOW THE MONEY MAP WORKS

Here's how to make the Crown Money Map (shown on next two pages) work for you. Review each destination on the journey to true financial freedom, and check off what you've already accomplished. Then, start with the first destination you have not yet finished. For example, you may have purchased your home but not paid off your credit cards. Check off the home purchase and then start at Destination Two, working to eliminate credit card debt. Complete each destination in order before proceeding to the next one.

As you can see, many of the destinations focus on becoming debt-free. For the remainder of this book, that is what we will help you do.

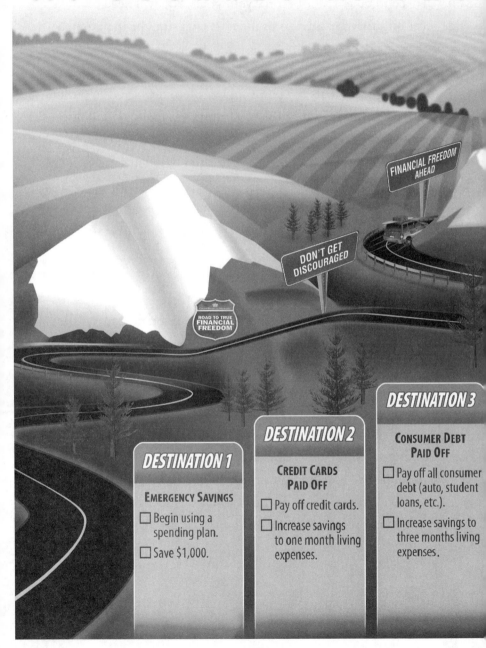

INANCIAL FREEDOM

TRUE FINANCIAL FREEDOM

DON'T QUIT
STAY FOCUSED
NOW

FINAL DESTINATION

☐ My retirement is funded.

☐ I am free to volunteer my time working for the Lord.

DESTINATION 6

HOME MORTGAGE PAID OFF

☐ Home mortgage paid off.

☐ Children's education funded.

☐ Confirm estate plan is in order.

DESTINATION 5

BUY HOME AND BEGIN INVESTING

☐ Buy affordable home.

☐ Begin prepaying home mortgage.

☐ Begin investing wisely.

DESTINATION 4

SAVE FOR MAJOR PURCHASES

☐ Begin saving for major purchases (home, auto, etc.).

☐ Begin saving for retirement.

☐ Begin saving for children's education.

☐ If you want to start your own business, begin saving.

CROWN FINANCIAL MINISTRIES

MONEY MAP

THE ASSIGNMENT

Tim was grinning. "I'm excited that this is designed so simply."

"But we've got so much debt that it isn't going to be easy," cautioned Cindy.

"Cindy's right," I agreed. "Like any journey, there will be bumps in the road and some hard decisions. But from personal experience we can tell you it's worth the effort and even the sacrifices you'll make. And I know that with the Lord's help, you can do it.

"Let's meet again in two weeks. I'm going to give you an assignment to complete and bring with you. First, identify your life purposes and short-term and long-term goals. Then complete this Personal Financial Statement and Debt List that I'll give you. They'll help you understand where you are financially."

TAKING STOCK

By now you're probably feeling more optimistic about your financial situation. I certainly hope so. That's usually what happens when people are first exposed to the Crown Money Map™. Please answer these two questions.

1. How do you feel about following the Money Map in your journey toward true financial freedom?

2. In what ways do you believe setting and writing down your financial goals will help you?

Now take some time to go through the process of discovering your life purpose. After you do, write it down either here or in some prominent place. Do the same if you're married, and write down what you determined for the life purpose of your marriage.

My Life Purpose:

Our Life Purpose for Our Marriage:

Perhaps before moving to the next chapter, you could visit the Crown Web site and see what else you can discover about the Money Map, which is indeed a helpful resource. Go to: www.crownfreeandclear. org.

Take the time to complete an estimated
spending plan . . . to get a firm grip
on the reality of your situation.

CHAPTER FIVE

Where **Are You?**

Acouple of weeks later Bev and I met with the Connors. Tim and Cindy were encouraged yet embarrassed.

"What did you learn about yourselves as you discussed your life purposes and goals?" I asked.

"It's the first time we really talked together about our dreams," Tim said. "I learned a lot about Cindy—and even myself. We think it's going to help a lot as we try to spend money on what's most important to us. But, unfortunately, we had a terrible argument."

"It was bad news," acknowledged Cindy as she blushed. "We didn't realize how much debt we had until we filled out the debt list you suggested we complete. We were completely overwhelmed by what it revealed. The reality of how hard it's going to be triggered a lot of emotion, and we didn't handle it well," she admitted.

"But the good news is that you now know the facts," I said. "Proverbs 24:3-4 says, *'Any enterprise is built by wise planning, becomes strong through common sense, and profits wonderfully by* keeping abreast of the facts' (emphasis mine, TLB). It's nearly impossible to make wise decisions without understanding the facts.

"Another reason I wanted you to complete a financial statement is to determine if there's anything you don't need that might be sold to help you get out of debt faster."

Tim quickly chimed in, "I've got a set of golf clubs and a woodworking machine in the garage that are just gathering dust. Let's sell them!"

"That's a good start, Tim." I nodded. "But don't stop. Ask yourselves the hard question about everything you have: Do we really need it? If not, consider selling it."

"We're also not exactly sure what interest rate we're being charged on some of our debts," Tim added. "How can we find that out?"

"That's now easy to figure out," I replied. "There's a law called *The Truth in Lending Act* that requires creditors to tell you the cost of borrowing in common language. By remembering one term, you'll understand what they're charging you. This will help decide which debts to pay off first, while making it easier to shop for the lowest rates. All creditors must tell you—in writing and before you sign any agreement—the *annual percentage rate.*

"The annual percentage rate (APR) is the percentage rate the lender charges figured on a yearly basis, including the cost of interest plus other costs, such as service charges. It measures the true cost of borrowing. For example, borrowing $1,000 for a year might cost $100 in interest. If there were a service charge of $5, the APR would be 10.5 percent.

"Now, let's take a look at your financial statement and debt list." Sheepishly, the Connors slid the papers across the table. They owed more than they owned, resulting in a negative net worth of $18,540. Their debts totaled $268,990, and their monthly payments were $2,585.

FINANCIAL STATEMENT
Tim and Cindy Connor

Assets (what I/we own)

Cash on hand/Checking account	$ 500
Savings	1,500
Stocks and bonds	1,500
Cash value of life insurance	0
Coins	0
Home	210,000
Other real estate	0
Mortgages/Notes receivable	0
Business valuation	0
Automobiles	20,100
Furniture	3,500
Jewelry	0
Other personal property	3,000
Pension/Retirement accounts	10,350
Other assets	0
Total Assets:	**$250,450**

Liabilities (what I/we owe)

Credit card debt	18,140
Automobile loans	22,350
Home mortgage	175,100
Other real estate mortgages	0
Debts to relatives	0
Business loans	0
Student loans	18,400
Medical/Past due bills	0
Life insurance loans	0
Bank loans	35,000
Other debts and loans	0
Total Liabilities:	**$268,990**

Net Worth (assets minus liabilities)   ($18,540)

DEBT LIST
Tim and Cindy Connor

Creditor	Debt	Monthly Payment	Interest Rate	Months Past Due (months)
Visa credit card	$ 5,770	$ 115	16%	0
MasterCard	4,250	100	14%	2
Visa credit card #2	5,950	120	11%	0
Department store card	1,620	80	16%	1
Gas credit card	500	30	14%	0
Cindy's car loan	7,550	160	7%	1
Tim's car loan	14,800	350	8%	0
Student loan	18,400	110	4%	0
Home equity loan	35,000	290	7%	0
Home mortgage	175,100	1,230	7%	0
Total	**$268,940**	**$2,585**		

Even a quick review of the Connors' situation shows how the numbers don't add up. This can lead to more and more stress if each month they get further in debt. Thankfully, there is always hope, the Connors learned. No matter what the situation, *no one* is beyond help.

FINDING HOPE

Crown Financial Ministries has worked with literally millions of people in similar circumstances. Our experience confirms that there is hope. We have repeatedly seen the Lord bless the efforts of those who faithfully apply His financial principles to their particular situation. It can be done.

Many people, particularly if they owe a lot, do not know exactly how much they owe. The tempting thought must be human nature: *If we avoid unpleasant things, perhaps they will go away.* However, no matter how you feel about your debts, you must list them in black and white to get the facts of your current financial situation. It's a necessary first step in creating the plan that will set you free.

There is a blank *Financial Statement* and a *Debt List* on the next two pages. If you haven't already completed one, don't put it off—it won't get any easier. Take the time now to complete them. Even getting your situation down on paper will bring a certain sense of genuine relief.

THE ASSIGNMENT

Thankfully, I was able to say to Tim and Cindy, "Well, I notice on your financial statement that you have $1,500 in savings for emergencies. That's awesome! You're halfway to Destination One on the Crown Money Map. Your next assignment will get you all the way there.

"I want you to keep track of every penny you both spend for the next thirty days. Carry some paper with you and write down *everything* you spend. Then get together each day to review what you spent and record it in a notebook. Begin each of these daily meetings by praying for the Lord's peace and for each other. As you know, this can be emotional. I want you to love and encourage each other through it.

"Finally, take the time to complete the estimated spending plan that I'll give you, and let's meet in a month to review it. Once you begin using a spending plan, you'll be ready to start the trip to Destination Two. I'm excited for you!"

The assignment I gave to Tim and Cindy is *your* assignment too. You need to get a firm grip on the reality of your situation. The only way to do that is to write everything down. Then you'll understand it clearly. Then you're ready to make some real progress down God's road toward debt-free living. As you turn the page, ask for the Lord's help and then trust Him for the results. Are you ready? Good for you!

FINANCIAL STATEMENT

Assets (what I/we own)
    Cash on hand/Checking account   _____
    Savings   _____
    Stocks and bonds   _____
    Cash value of life insurance   _____
    Coins   _____
    Home   _____
    Other real estate   _____
    Mortgages/Notes receivable   _____
    Business valuation   _____
    Automobiles   _____
    Furniture   _____
    Jewelry   _____
    Other personal property   _____
    Pension/Retirement accounts   _____
    Other assets   _____
Total Assets: _____

Liabilities (what I/we owe)
    Credit card debt   _____
    Automobile loans   _____
    Home mortgage   _____
    Other real estate mortgages   _____
    Debts to relatives   _____
    Business loans   _____
    Educational loans   _____
    Medical/Past due bills   _____
    Life insurance loans   _____
    Bank loans   _____
    Other debts and loans   _____
Total Liabilities: _____

Net Worth (assets minus liabilities)   _____

DEBT LIST

Creditor	Debt	Monthly Payment	Interest Rate	Months Past Due (months)
Credit card #1	$_____	$_____	_____	_____
Credit card #2	_____	_____	_____	_____
Credit card #3	_____	_____	_____	_____
Credit card #4	_____	_____	_____	_____
Credit card #5	_____	_____	_____	_____
Credit card #6	_____	_____	_____	_____
Car loan #1	_____	_____	_____	_____
Car loan #2	_____	_____	_____	_____
Student loan	_____	_____	_____	_____
Home equity loan	_____	_____	_____	_____
Home mortgage	_____	_____	_____	_____
Other real estate debt	_____	_____	_____	_____
Debts to relatives	_____	_____	_____	_____
Business loans	_____	_____	_____	_____
Medical/Past due bills	_____	_____	_____	_____
Other debts	_____	_____	_____	_____
Total Debts	$_____	$_____		

TAKING STOCK

Hopefully, this chapter was a reality check for you—a check that does not discourage you but helps to move you forward in your plan.

1. In what ways has writing the details of your situation motivated you for the journey?

2. What emotions did you feel as you went through the process?

Relief   *Frustration*   *Anger*   *Guilt*

3. Complete this sentence: *Now that I know where I am financially . . .*

_____

_____

_____

_____.

Ask yourself two questions about *every* expense: Can I do this less expensively? Do I really need this?

CHAPTER SIX

Acting Your Own Wage

Have you got a few minutes? We're in bigger trouble than we thought," Tim began. Tim and Cindy had unexpectedly dropped by my office. Fearing bad news, I locked eyes with Tim.

As he began to open his mouth, Cindy, in near panic, blurted, "We're spending almost $600 more every month than our income. No wonder our debt's out of control!"

"When we last met," I reassured them, "we talked about how important it is to get the facts. Remember how upset you were after discovering what you owned and what you owed? Now, you've found out what you're really earning and spending.

"I remember warning you that you might be frustrated by what the spending plan reveals. Most people have no idea that the average person in our country spends $1.10 for every dollar earned. The first draft of a spending plan usually has more outgo than income. *But take heart—there's hope!* I believe you can make adjustments and balance it. Let's take a look at your spending plan."

Tim and Cindy put their spending plan before me. It's shown on the next page.

"Hmmmm, I think I can see some areas where you can cut expenses," I said. "However, I'm very encouraged that you are giving generously to the Lord's work. It's important to tithe; give 10 percent. Although I know it's a real stretch for you and is counterintuitive, generosity is one of the keys in becoming debt-free. Acts 20:35 reads, *'Remembering the words the Lord Jesus himself said: "It is more blessed to give than to receive."'* One blessing for those who are generous is that the Lord has more freedom to intervene in their finances."

THE FREEDOM OF A SPENDING PLAN

I don't like to use the "B" word because so many people think of a *budget* as a restrictive loss of freedom. They also fear a budget requires endless hours of monotonous, detailed accounting.

A *spending plan,* however, is a more accurate description. It tells your money where you want it to go rather than wondering where it went. It enables you to use your money to reach your goals and life purpose. It helps you control impulse spending and get out of debt. That's why the Connors agreed they needed a spending plan.

If you are not using a spending plan, chances are you are flying by the seat of your financial pants. You may be like the depositor who replied in disbelief to the banker, "What do you mean I'm overdrawn? I still have six checks left in my checkbook!" Talk about a reality check! Sometimes adjustments are in order.

MONTHLY SPENDING PLAN
Tim and Cindy Connor

Total Income	4,899	**Entertainment/Recreation**		142
Salary	4,889	Eating out		67
Interest	5	Babysitters		0
Dividends	5	Activities/Trips		10
Other income		Vacation		50
Less		Pets		15
* Giving/Tithe	490			
* Taxes	835	**Clothing**		92
Spendable Income	3,574	**Savings**		0
		Medical		40
Living Expenses		Doctor		20
Housing	1,540	Dentist		10
Mortgage or rent	1,230	Prescriptions		10
Insurance	43	Other		0
Property taxes	60			
Electricity	62	**Miscellaneous**		155
Cable TV	40	Toiletries/Cosmetics		16
Gas	12	Beauty/Barber		31
Water	8	Laundry/Cleaning		12
Sanitation	10	Allowances		36
Telephone	25	Subscriptions		20
Maintenance	50	Gifts		40
Other	0	Other		0
Food	412	**School/Child care**		216
		Tuition		200
Transportation	715	Materials		16
Payments	510	Transportation		0
Gas & oil	55	Day care		0
Insurance	45			
License/Taxes	25	**Investments**		0
Maint./Replace	80			
Other	0	**Living Expenses**		4,120
Insurance	73	*How the Month Turns Out*		
Life	30	Spendable income		3,574
Health	43	Minus living expenses		4,120
Other	0	Monthly surplus or deficit		(546)
Debts	735			
(except auto & house)				

ADJUSTMENTS TO YOUR SPENDING PLAN

If you are spending more than your income or if you want to accelerate your debt repayment, you must ask yourself two questions about *every* expense: Can I do this less expensively? Do I really need this?

Reducing spending means you must change your lifestyle. This is never easy. Tim and Cindy made hard decisions because of their commitment to get out of debt. They canceled their cable TV, stopped magazine subscriptions, and sold the auto with the higher car loan. They made big cuts and small ones. They enrolled their children in public school and were careful in the use of electricity.

The Connors' spending plan improved from a monthly deficit of $546 to a surplus of $210. They were in a position to begin paying off their debts. Again, the principle is true: Discovering where you are motivates you toward progress.

YOUR SPENDING PLAN: THINGS TO KEEP IN MIND

You May Need a Coach

Many people discover that it's too difficult to start and sustain a spending plan without help. They need advice, encouragement, and accountability from someone who is successfully using one. We recommend that you ask someone experienced for assistance. You may have a close relative or a friend who is successful at managing money. Or you might consult your pastor for suggestions. If you do not know such a person, contact Crown online at: www.crownfreeandclear.org for the name of a volunteer in your area trained in setting up spending plans.

The Challenge of Unpredictable Income

Some people who receive their income from self-employment or sales commissions argue that they can't use a spending plan because their income is unpredictable. That issue simply magnifies the importance of using one. If your income is not consistent, estimate your yearly income and divide it by twelve to determine your average monthly income.

Work toward establishing a savings reserve from which you can draw steady income. For example, assume you are able to save $4,000 for this reserve, and your spending plan requires $3,000 income per month. If you earn $2,000 during a month, withdraw $1,000 from savings to meet your expenses. If you earn $5,000 the next month, spend only the planned $3,000 and deposit the rest into the savings reserve. The biggest challenge for those with unpredictable incomes is not to spend *everything* they earn during higher income months.

The Reality of Variable Expenses

To establish an accurate spending plan, you need to be able to account for spending that varies each month. These include utility bills, food, clothing, house and auto repairs, etc. Estimate the average monthly cost for each category by determining the annual amount and dividing by twelve.

Different Strokes for Different Folks

When it comes to using a spending plan, there are many effective methods; choose the one best suited for you. There are four basic systems:

1. *The envelope system.* This is the way many of our grandparents planned their spending, and it still works. When the paycheck came, it was cashed and the money was distributed among various spending categories and deposited in

envelopes. And when the clothing envelope was empty, no more was spent on clothes.

2. *Pencil and paper.* Many people prefer using a standard checkbook and ledger system.

3. *Budgeting software.* Many reasonably priced, user-friendly software programs are available that can help you manage your personal finances.

4. *Online, wireless budgeting.* A growing number of people are using powerful and secure budgeting systems connected to the Internet.

The key is to find a system you are comfortable using. For recommendations, visit crownfreeandclear.org or check with a friend who uses a reliable product.

The Teamwork of Husband and Wife

Husbands and wives should work together on developing their initial spending plan, engaging in open, honest communication as they do. The Lord intended the husband and wife to be unified, which is why He said in Genesis 2:24, *"A man will leave . . . and be united to his wife, and they will become one flesh."* Be patient with each other and your different personalities and approaches to money. Men often like to "get things done" quickly. Women tend to need time to process and discuss. The key is flexibility and honesty. Don't rush the process. The hard work now will pay huge dividends later.

Once you have drawn up your initial spending plan, the spouse more gifted (that's code for "organized"!) in keeping records should do the accounting. Then, meet together once a week to examine your progress, discuss challenges, and make needed adjustments.

Couples who want the wife to stay home while children are

young should design their spending plan based on only the husband's income. If she works in advance of that, use her income for debt reduction and savings. The less you are obligated to pay each month on debt, the easier it will be to transition to a stay-at-home mom.

Taking the Woes Out of Ho, Ho, Ho!

One of the biggest budget busters is unbridled spending for Christmas, birthdays, and other celebrations. Do not underestimate this; it is a real problem for many, especially if you have children. A recent survey discovered that the biggest fear people have at Christmastime is managing the after-Christmas debt! The bills that follow the spending binge send many people into depression. It does not have to be that way.

The key is establishing a strict budget—yes, I used the "B" word in this case! Your spending for gifts needs to be carefully controlled. Even people with average creativity—if they put their minds to it —can make or buy personalized gifts that are not expensive. The value is in their uniqueness and the way they fit the recipients, reflecting their personal interests. If you have a large extended family, consider getting everyone together and deciding on a name-swapping system. That way you're only buying gifts for one or two family members and not the whole clan! You get the picture. Give it some thought and be creative now and you'll save yourself much money . . . and heartache . . . later.

Gambling and Compulsive Spending

If you have a problem with gambling or compulsive spending, it is crucial for you to admit it. You should not be embarrassed, because there are millions of people wrestling with the same thing. However, you do need help!

Become a member of a Christ-centered support group. Address this issue for your financial and emotional health and for the sake of your loved ones. Visit www.crownfreeandclear.org for links to helpful resources.

THE ASSIGNMENT

In the same way, writing down the details of your current situation motivated you toward progress, developing a spending plan will bring structure to your decision to become debt-free. I urge you not to skip this process. Don't try to keep everything in your head or on a napkin or scrap piece of paper. Use the form provided on the next page to get you on your way to controlling your spending and eradicating your debt.

MONTHLY SPENDING PLAN

Total Income _____
Salary _____
Interest _____
Dividends _____
Other income _____
Less
   * Giving/Tithe _____
   * Taxes _____

Spendable Income _____

Living Expenses
Housing
   Mortgage or rent _____
   Insurance _____
   Property taxes _____
   Electricity _____
   Cable TV _____
   Gas _____
   Water _____
   Sanitation _____
   Telephone _____
   Maintenance _____
   Other _____

Food _____

Transportation _____
   Payments _____
   Gas & oil _____
   Insurance _____
   License/Taxes _____
   Maint./Replace _____
   Other _____

Insurance _____
   Life _____
   Health _____
   Other _____

Debts _____
(except auto & house)

Entertainment/Recreation _____
   Eating out _____
   Babysitters _____
   Activities/Trips _____
   Vacation _____
   Pets _____

Clothing _____

Savings _____

Medical _____
   Doctor _____
   Dentist _____
   Prescriptions _____
   Other _____

Miscellaneous
   Toiletries/Cosmetics _____
   Beauty/Barber _____
   Laundry/Cleaning _____
   Allowances _____
   Subscriptions _____
   Gifts _____
   Other _____

School/Child care _____
   Tuition _____
   Materials _____
   Transportation _____
   Day care _____

Investments _____

Living Expenses _____

How the Month Turns Out
Spendable income _____
Minus living expenses _____
Monthly surplus or deficit _____

TAKING STOCK

Whew! That's some heavy lifting, isn't it? Well, believe me, you'll never regret taking the time to get your spending plan settled and in writing. Good for you.

1. How do you feel about the results?

2. What was the most rewarding aspect of going through the process of setting up your spending plan?

3. Take some time to thank the Lord for His help in giving you the patience and wisdom to complete this important task. I know He is pleased with your progress too!

Much of the battle to become debt-free takes place in your mind. You need to remind yourself constantly of the goal.

CHAPTER SEVEN

Your Mind Over Money

Bev wanted to share with Tim and Cindy what she considered her most important step in becoming free from the bondage of debt. So one Saturday afternoon the four of us met at the city park.

"I've struggled with my weight for more than fifteen years," Bev confided.

"Well, you could have fooled me!" Cindy responded, shaking her head in disbelief. "You look so slim."

Bev smiled. "You wouldn't have said that several years ago. I've lost more than fifty pounds."

"How much?" Cindy asked in amazement. "How did you do it? Did you go on a radical diet or something?"

"No, I've tried dozens of diets," Bev confessed. "But nothing worked for long. Then we met a couple; each of them had lost fifteen pounds by going on a reasonable diet. Well, it wasn't a diet so much as a healthy way of eating. And it just made sense. The secret of their success was that they developed a mind-set of eating in a healthy way that would allow them to control their weight.

"So first I looked at what the Bible said about our bodies. First Corinthians 3:16 says, 'Don't you know that you yourselves are God's temple and that God's Spirit lives in you?' I meditated on this passage and came to understand that the Lord lives in my body and that I need to be faithful to take care of it.

"Then I prayed that the Lord would give me the mental discipline to begin eating wisely for both weight loss and overall health. Next, I established a goal for how much I wanted to lose. Then I joined a gym and started to work out regularly to burn more calories. And it definitely helped when Howard agreed to eat the same way.

"I weighed myself once a week to gauge progress, knowing that some weeks I would lose and other weeks I'd gain a little. I stayed encouraged by reading helpful books, and I even led a class of women who wanted to lose weight.

"One other important thing that gave me strength and helped keep my eye on the goal: I memorized several Bible verses and a few rhymes that I would recite whenever I felt tempted to eat something I shouldn't.'"

As Bev told her story, all kinds of memories filled my mind. "That's right," I said, smiling. "I've heard those rhymes so often I can repeat them: 'Nothing tastes as good as slim feels.' 'Ten seconds on the lips means ten pounds on the hips.' 'If you don't need it, don't eat it.' Bev was successful because she developed the mind-set to lose weight and no temptation would keep her from reaching her goal."

Tim and Cindy admitted they had never thought about how developing a proper mind-set could help them reach their financial goals. But Bev and I are convinced that this discipline is a critical step for anyone wanting to climb out of debt and stay out.

THE DEBT-FREE MIND-SET

I want to share with you several disciplines that will help you overcome debt and get on the road to financial freedom. Each one is equally important in developing a debt-free mind-set.

Meditate

Select several Bible passages that deal with God's perspective on debt. I suggest two verses that we looked at in chapter 3:

> *Let no debt remain outstanding.* (Romans 13:8)
> *The borrower is servant to the lender.* (Proverbs 22:7)

Memorize those two verses. Meditate on them by saying them over and over in your mind, especially when you feel tempted to use debt. Bringing these Bible verses to your mind in those times will give you the strength to resist the temptation. That's how God's Word begins to produce in you a passion to become debt-free.

Pray

Each day ask the Lord to give you the necessary insight, discipline, and persistence to pay off your debt. Some people are reluctant to pray for God's help with their debt because they feel guilty about having incurred it. They wonder whether it would be legitimate to ask God to help them out of a mess they created themselves. Others think that handling money is not really a spiritual issue, so God wouldn't be interested. Though I do understand those feelings, nothing could be further from the truth. God cares deeply about you and whatever financial dilemma you find yourself facing—and He desires for you to be free.

Remember Philippians 4:6–7: *"Do not be anxious about anything, but in* everything, *by prayer and petition, with thanksgiving, present your requests to God"* (emphasis added). You're to pray about everything. The Lord wants to be involved in every area of your life. And He desires for you to know Him well and discover how deeply He loves you. In your effort to get rid of debt, there is nothing more important than asking for the Lord's assistance.

Establish the Goal and Go for It!

Set the goal of becoming debt-free. Try to be as specific as possible. Then write everything down. Remember what Bev did to reach her goal.

1. *Look at the facts.* She stepped on the scales once a week to monitor her progress. The scales told her the truth about how well she was doing. This is the reason it is important to develop a spending plan and debt list. Keep them current and review them at least once a week.

2. *Accelerate the goal.* Do you remember what Bev did to lose weight more rapidly? She started exercising at the gym. If you can earn even a little more money to use against your debts, it is amazing how much faster D-day—Debtless Day—will happen.

3. *Involve your spouse.* If you are married, it makes all the difference when you and your spouse are working together to become debt-free. Mark 3:25 says, *"If a house is divided against itself, that house cannot stand."* You and your mate must be on the same page regarding your debt reduction. It's essential if you are going to become completely free. I suggest you meet regularly together to pray, review the facts, discuss how to improve, and celebrate the victories, no matter how small. Use your times of prayer as an opportunity to grow closer together as a couple.

Overcome Discouragement and Temptation

The journey to freedom from debt is not easy. At times you may want to quit because it is too hard, or the temptation to spend is too great. Bev faced those same temptations while trying to lose weight many times because she *loves* chocolate. But she realized that if she gave in to her desires, her dream of losing weight would remain just that—a dream. The real battle was in her mind.

That is when she would remind herself, "Nothing tastes as good as slim feels." "Ten seconds on the lips means ten pounds on the hips." "If I don't need it, I won't eat it."

I want you to write down these statements—or create your own—and carry them with you:

> "Nothing I buy feels as good as being debt-free."
> "Ten seconds to use my credit card, ten months to pay it off."
> "If I don't need it, I won't buy it."

Much of the battle to become debt-free takes place in your mind. You need to remind yourself constantly of the goal. It has to become more important to you than spending money on things you really do not need. No matter your situation, you can do it with God's help.

WATCH OUT! THEY WANT YOUR MONEY

You need to know that you're going up against marketing and advertising professionals who are paid mind-boggling salaries to separate you from your money. Your efforts to get out of debt are especially challenging because you live in the biggest consumer society in all of history. Why are billions of advertising dollars spent every day in our country? There is only one reason—companies want your money! Everywhere you turn, someone is pitching their stuff. Television, radio, the Internet, billboards, newspapers, magazines, shopping malls—the list goes on and on. You are exposed to thousands of messages each day to spend more and more.

Advertisers have become incredibly sophisticated in their techniques to induce you to spend. They invest millions on surveys, focus groups, and testing strategies to determine the most effective ways to hook you into buying their stuff. They spend a fortune choosing the best name, the best colors, and the most emotionally powerful images to market their products. And they don't care if you spend money you don't have!

When you try to beat them at their own game, it is almost impossible to win. It's the amateur versus the professionals, and guess who's the amateur? You! The only way you can win is to ask the Lord to give you the discipline to limit your exposure to the enticing ads and tantalizing stores and products being offered at every turn. Ask God to form within you the mind-set that says, "Nothing I buy feels as good as being debt-free." He'll do it, if you ask Him.

HOW TO RESIST THE PITCH

Now let me offer you a three-point strategy to help you stand firm against the relentless onslaught of advertising.

1. Limit your exposure.

It seems almost un-American in this "Shop 'til you drop" society, but one of the most effective ways to bring spending under control is to isolate yourself from the temptations. Bev came to understand that if she was to meet her weight-loss goal, she could not afford to go into an ice cream shop; her favorite double-chocolate ice cream dish would be just too great a temptation. The same is true for controlling your spending.

We've all had a similar experience of going shopping to buy one item and then leaving the store or Web site with lots of other things we stumble across. So the key is to limit your exposure. Here are three truisms:

- The more television you watch, the more you spend.
- The more you look at catalogs and magazines and Internet retail sites, the more you spend.
- The more you shop, the more you spend.

By the way, with the proliferation of Internet shopping, you *must* limit your exposure to online shopping opportunities. Amazon.com, Ebay, and countless other Web-based retailers are cool and convenient places to visit. But they also represent opportunities to easily spend more than you have because you have to pay by using plastic in most cases. So limit your Internet shopping.

2. Cultivate contentment.

Frequently, our culture tries to create in us discontentment with what we have. Keeping up with the Joneses has become a national pastime. As someone once said, "Just about the time you've caught up with the Joneses, they refinance their house and buy a bunch more stuff." Our consumption-oriented society operates on the assumption that happiness comes from stuff, and more is always better. The result? Widespread discontentment.

In sharp contrast, the Lord wants you to experience contentment. The word *contentment* is mentioned seven times in Scripture, and six times it has to do with handling money and possessions.

Jesus said it most plainly: *"A man's life does not consist in the abundance of his possessions"* (Luke 12:15). The apostle Paul also wrote about contentment: *"I have learned to be content whatever the circumstances. I know what it is to be in need, and I know what it is to have plenty. I have learned the secret of being content in any and every situation, whether well fed or hungry, whether living in plenty or in want. I can do everything through him who gives me strength"* (Philippians 4:11–13).

Paul "learned" to be content. No one is born with the instinct of contentment; rather, it's a quality we must learn to develop.

Real contentment enables us to live within our means. It values the true riches of a relationship with the Lord, family, and friends. It resists the urge to buy the next big thing simply because we can charge it. Contentment means gladly accepting our present situation as adequate. The need for more is diminished.

3. Pray for the Lord to provide.

When Bev and I first determined that God wanted us completely out of debt, we decided that we would pray and wait for the Lord to provide things rather than run out and charge them.

Today as we walk around our home, we are overwhelmed as we look together at all the items the Lord has provided. There was the gift of our dining room table and chairs, the $3 solid-oak chair from a garage sale, and our bed's headboard—an item for which we waited ten years.

Most of the furnishings in our home have a similar story. We enjoy them for many reasons, but the biggest is that they are tangible reminders of God's love, faithfulness, and provision.

Your number one resource for getting out of debt is the Lord. He is able to accomplish what you desire. And He waits willingly and patiently for you to ask for His help. He's ready when you are!

TAKING STOCK

1. What did you discover in this chapter about the importance of your mind-set to control your spending?

2. In what ways is your current mind-set helping or hindering you from getting on the road to true financial freedom? Explain.

3. How do you feel about meditating on Bible verses? In the space below, write down two or three verses that you believe will be a source of encouragement for you.

Passage 1:

Passage 2:

Passage 3:

Your credit score affects the interest rates you pay and your long-term financial future. Being faithful in reducing your debt and paying your bills on time will . . . improve your score.

CHAPTER EIGHT

Credit Scores
and Credit Reports

Tim Connor had been reviewing his credit card statements of the past two years. He wasn't happy about what he discovered.

"I can't believe these credit card companies have jacked up our interest rates *seven* times in just two years!" he said, his face flushed with anger. "Why did they do it? They didn't even bother to tell us."

Cindy's expression was tinged with guilt as she looked at me. "Well, we missed payments now and then, and other times we were late. Would that have anything to do with it?"

"That could have done it," I agreed. "Some lenders constantly monitor credit scores. And when the scores drop, it's not unusual for them to increase your interest rates. And they're not obligated to notify you. It happens all the time. Credit reports and credit scores play a bigger role than most people realize."

This conversation reflects what millions of Americans

experience every day. People simply are unaware of the importance of their credit scores and feel helpless in managing their impact. If you are to be successful on your journey toward becoming debt-free, it will be vital to become familiar with this critical element of your financial situation.

UNDERSTANDING YOUR CREDIT SCORE

Why Your Credit Score Is Important

Did you know that credit scores determine whether you can get credit extended to you? That credit includes loans for a car, appliances, a credit card, and even a mortgage. At times, your credit score can even impact the amount required for a utility deposit. Also, your score may be high enough to get credit but not high enough to get a decent interest rate, causing your application to rent an apartment to be turned down or your car insurance premiums to rise. In some cases, a low credit score may impact your ability to get a job. So understanding how a credit score works can help to change your financial future.

What Is a Credit Score?

A credit score is a number designed to help lenders and others measure your likelihood of making timely payments. The Fair Isaac Corporation developed the FICO score formula, which ranges from 300–850, with the average score being around 680. The higher your score, the better off you are. FICO scores above 700 indicate a good credit risk, while scores below 600 indicate a poor risk.

A low score can lead to *much* higher interest rates or even a rejected loan application. For example, if you apply for a thirty-year home mortgage and your credit score is 720, you will get a favorable interest rate, in most cases. But if your score is 580, you could pay as much as 3 percent more. On a $100,000 mortgage, that 3 percent difference will cost you $200 per month or $2,400 a year. Over the life of the loan it adds up to $72,000. That's real money!

Now, this is important to understand: Credit scores are based on the information contained in your credit report. The report does not contain any personal information unrelated to credit, such as your race, medical history, and religious preference. Receiving food stamps or public assistance will not affect the score, nor will the amount of money you earn. Your credit report cares only about your credit history; the premise is that your past handling of debt is the most reliable guide to what you will do with new credit.

Factors Affecting Your FICO Credit Score

Five factors from your credit report influence your score.

1. *Your payment history* (about 35 percent of score). Have you paid your bills on time? On-time payments increase your score; late payments lower it.
2. *How much you owe* (about 30 percent). FICO scores take into consideration the amount of debt you owe, the number of accounts with balances due, and how much of your available credit line you are using. The more you owe, the lower the score.
3. *Length of history* (about 15 percent). A longer credit history translates into a higher score, but even a shorter history can be positive as long as it shows consistent on-time payments.
4. *New credit* (about 10 percent). If you have recently applied for or opened new credit accounts, your credit score may reflect that activity. Every application shows up as an

inquiry, hinting you may be seeking credit that would overextend your ability to repay. Generally, if you need a loan, shop for the loan in a short time frame, such as thirty days, to avoid harming your credit score from too many inquiries.

5. *Other issues* (about 10 percent). Several other factors such as the mix of debt types you carry—credit cards, auto loan, and home mortgage—may also slightly impact your score.

How Your Credit Score Is Lowered

Your credit score is so important that I want to make sure you understand the primary things that will harm it:

- Any late payments or nonpayments of bills or debts. Once you go beyond thirty-days past due on any credit account, the credit scoring agencies are automatically notified. The delinquent status shows up on your score.
- High outstanding debt compared with your credit limits. Those who have maxed out their credit limits are considered higher risk for future nonpayment.
- Bankruptcy or financial judgments against you. Bills or loans sent to collection will also lower your credit score.
- Foreclosure on mortgages. Repossession of anything you have purchased on credit, such as autos, boats, and campers.
- Too short a credit history.
- Too many open accounts or applications. If you have a very large amount of credit readily available, there is the possibility that you could use it and overextend yourself. Apply for new credit accounts only when you need them.

You may be surprised to discover just how many factors weigh in on your credit score. And you're likely beginning to see just how critical it is to your financial future. Thankfully, you can improve your score using some strategies that, if put in place now, will over time yield positive results. You can improve your score!

IMPROVING YOUR CREDIT SCORE

To improve your credit score, the two most important actions you can take are to pay your bills on time and reduce your total debt. It's that simple. Once you start doing that, your score will begin to improve in about three months.

One suggestion: If you have difficulty paying your bills on time because of lack of discipline, arrange for an automatic monthly electronic funds transfer from your account to cover the minimum amounts due.

Most negative information does not disappear overnight; it takes time to repair the damage. Late or missed payments and events of public record, such as foreclosure or repossession, remain part of your credit report for seven years. You'll have to wait ten years for a bankruptcy to be removed, and fifteen years for a tax lien.

Even though these remain on your credit report, over time they have less impact if you pay your bills on time and reduce your debt. If you ever consider bankruptcy, foreclosure, or repossession, realize it will affect you for years.

YOUR CREDIT REPORT

Everyone should get a copy of their credit report once a year. Review it to make sure there are no mistakes. The three nationwide consumer reporting companies (TransUnion, Equifax, and Experian) have set up one central Web site and toll-free telephone number through which you can order a free copy of your credit report once every twelve months. To order, click on www.annualcreditreport.com or call toll-free (877) 322-8228. Do not contact the three companies directly for your free annual report; they provide them only through the central Web site and toll-free number.

Keep in mind that you can receive a free report from *each* agency. This feature means if you spread out your requests during the year, you can monitor one of your credit reports every four months. This helps you monitor potential identity theft and detect errors on your reports throughout the year.

Although you have the right to receive a free copy of your credit reports once a year, none of your three reports shows your score. Unless you are applying for a home mortgage or home equity loan, you will have to pay to receive your credit score. Each of the three main credit agencies keeps its own score, and the scores vary slightly. Any of them will sell you your score or you can purchase all three scores from www.myfico.com.

To look at a sample credit report, go to www.crownfreeandclear.org and follow the link provided, so you can become familiar with the various aspects of this important tool.

Once you've received a copy of your credit report, take some time to study it carefully. Make certain all the information is accurate and that any open accounts are those you recall opening. Addresses and partial account numbers are provided for you to check against your records. Any accounts that are listed as still open or inactive can be closed. This may also have a positive impact on your overall score. If you find any errors, you are able to dispute that information.

If you have an unresolved dispute with any of your creditors, contact the credit reporting agency and tell your side of the story. They, in turn, will contact the creditor directly. The creditor has thirty days to respond and document their claim against you. If they do not respond, the item in dispute is removed from your credit report.

THE FAIR CREDIT REPORTING ACT

The U.S. Congress passed the Fair Credit Reporting Act to protect consumers against the circulation of inaccurate information and to ensure that credit reporting companies use fair procedures for obtaining and giving out information about consumers.

Under this law, you can take steps to protect yourself if you have been denied credit, insurance, or employment, or if you believe you have had difficulties because of an inaccurate or unfair credit report.

Questions or complaints should be directed to the Federal Trade Commission. For more information visit: www.ftc.gov.

GOING FORWARD

My best advice is to stay current with your credit report. Among other things, it will help you uncover identity theft if you ever become a victim. And remember, your credit score affects the interest rates you pay and your long-term financial future. When you are faithful in reducing your debt and paying your bills on time, you will not only improve your score but also move closer to becoming free and clear of your debt. This is one of the key steps on your journey to true financial freedom.

TAKING STOCK

Staying on top of your credit report is critical discipline as you journey toward true financial freedom. But let me emphasize: Don't become discouraged with the process. There is a road out, and God will help you every step of the way. He is bigger than a low credit score and not intimidated by the often frustrating process of communicating with creditors and agencies. He will work on your behalf, He really will!

Take some time before you move ahead to pause in prayer and thank the Lord for His help.

Hey, you're doing great. Stay at it. You'll be so glad you did!

If you consistently work to reduce your debt load, your momentum of paying down the principal on your balance builds to an exciting level. I call this the *Snowball Principle.*

CHAPTER NINE

The **Snowball**

im and Cindy Connor invited us over to their home. They took out their Crown Money Map and pointed to Destination Two, "Paying off Your Credit Cards." With real resolve, Cindy said, "We want to get here as soon as we can. How do we decide which credit card to pay off first?"

"Imagine that both of you together have decided to build a large snowman," I answered.

"You start with a small snowball the size of your hand, which you roll in the snow. The first rotation of the snowball picks up just a little extra snow. You can hardly tell it's grown in size. But you don't stop rolling it over. You don't give up.

"You roll it over a second time and this time it collects more snow. Encouraged, you continue pushing together. Three turns . . . four . . . five . . . six . . . seven . . . you keep pushing . . . eight . . . nine . . . ten. The snowball grows larger and larger with each turn.

"Now, the size and momentum of the snowball begin working

for you. Every time you roll the snowball over, it grows increasingly larger with each rotation."

The further I explained the concept of the snowball, the more Tim and Cindy smiled. They were starting to get the picture. Over time, if you are faithful to consistently work to reduce your debt load, your momentum of paying down the principal on your balance builds to an exciting level.

I call this increasing momentum the *Snowball Principle.* Actually, there are several principles associated with the powerful concept known as the Snowball Principle.

THE SNOWBALL PRINCIPLE

The snowball illustrates three key principles of paying off debt.

1. If you are married, both spouses must push in the same direction.

To maximize your progress, husband and wife must agree and work together to become debt-free. This goes back to the goals you set together relating to your financial future. I suggest you write what you're agreeing to down on paper, even date it, if you'd like. That seals it in both your minds and ensures you'll be pushing hard in the same direction.

2. The initial effort is usually the most challenging.

Normally, it is not easy to become debt-free. You must be consistent month after month in your journey toward D-Day—Debtless Day. The harder and more consistently you push against the snowball of your principal paydown, the faster your momentum will increase. God promises to honor consistent financial diligence. Proverbs 21:5 promises that *"the plans of the diligent lead to profit."* Discipline and diligence always brings reward.

3. The more you pay off debt, the more momentum you gain.

This is important to understand: You pay interest only on the *unpaid principal* balance. The faster you pay down your principal balance, the less you'll be paying in interest each month. As your principal decreases, fewer and fewer dollars from your monthly payment will be required to pay interest. More dollars each month will go toward paying down the principal.

Look at Cindy and Tim's loan repayment schedule for their major credit card. They owe $4,250 at 14 percent interest with monthly payments of $100.

Month	Payment	Interest	Principal	Principal Balance
January	$100.00	$49.58	$50.42	$4,199.58
February	100.00	49.00	51.00	4,148.58
March	100.00	48.40	51.60	4,096.98
April	100.00	47.80	52.20	4,044.78
May	100.00	47.19	52.81	3,991.97
June	100.00	46.57	53.43	3,938.54

As their payment each month reduces the unpaid principal balance, less interest is charged the following month. Just like the snowball, with each rotation—a monthly payment of $100—the results are greater; more of the payment is applied to reducing principal. It starts out slowly and steadily picks up momentum until—the snowball becomes huge! By the time the Connors owe $500 on this debt, only $5.83 will go toward interest while $94.17 will go to reduce principal.

THE SNOWBALL STRATEGY

Here's a step-by-step strategy for you to put the snowball principle in place for you and your situation. Following these steps consistently will produce dramatic results.

Pay off your smallest high-interest debt first.

Review the debt list you completed on page 51. In addition to making the minimum payments on all your debts, focus on accelerating the payment of your smallest high-interest debt first. You will be encouraged as you make progress, finally eliminating that debt.

Then, after you pay off the first debt, apply its payment toward the next smallest debt. After the second debt is paid off, apply what you were paying on the first and second debts toward the third smallest debt, and so forth. You will begin to dramatically improve your situation.

Tim and Cindy's smallest high-interest debt was a $500 gasoline company credit card bill. They had been paying $30 a month toward this debt and were able to increase this to $175, paying it off completely in three months.

Then, the Connors selected the second debt they wanted to eliminate—their $1,620 department store card. They had been paying $120 a month on this bill. So they added to this $120 the $175 they had been paying on the gas company card, retiring the department store debt in six months. That's the snowball principle in action! But it doesn't stop there.

Accelerate the Snowball

Once Bev and I started to snowball our debt, we got excited. We realized that if we could push a little harder against the snowball, we would pay off our debts much faster. We thought of a couple of simple ideas to help increase the amount of money we could apply to paying off debt. Here are just two suggestions.

First, sell things you no longer need. Bev and I decided to sell things we didn't really need, applying the sales proceeds to our debt. We did this through garage sales scheduled during times of the year when shoppers

were on the move! Also, we know of people who have used the www.
ebay.com Web site to sell their unwanted stuff. Whatever dollars you earn
by selling, apply them to your debt repayment immediately.

Many people have discovered they had cars, homes, or other
items they really couldn't afford. The payments on these were straining
their spending plan and not allowing them to push the debt-snowball
forward. If this is true in your case, I suggest downsizing—own less
and live simpler. Sell those items you don't really need as well as those
items you can't afford.

The money you were applying toward making those hefty
payments can now be applied to wiping out your other debts.

Second, apply any additional income to paying down debt. Bev and
I also knew we could accelerate the debt-snowball if we increased our
income and *applied it against our debt.* We committed in advance to use
additional income to knock out debt. That was important because
most of us tend to spend a little more than we make, whether we earn
a lot or a little. Spending always seems to stay ahead of income. By
adding income dollars to your debt repayment, you can crank up the
momentum of the snowball.

DEBT REPAYMENT SCHEDULE

I recommend you prepare a debt repayment schedule for every debt
that you focus on paying off early. It will help you stay on top of your
progress. For links to automated debt repayment computations, visit
www.crownfreeandclear.org. Also, you may wish to engage the help of
a volunteer Money Map coach. You can find one in your area also by
visiting the Crown Web site.

TAKING STOCK

1. How do you feel right now about your prospect of becoming totally debt-free?

2. What excites you the most about the thought of getting completely free and clear of debt?

By now I hope you're beginning to believe you really can become debt-free. What it takes is a firm resolve and a sound plan. God honors both. The Bible says this about making plans: *"Commit to the LORD whatever you do, and your plans will succeed"* (Proverbs 16:3).

3. Once you've established your debt repayment plan, take some time to commit it to the Lord. Ask for His help and then watch Him work.

Always take the initiative in keeping your lenders informed. When you communicate with your lenders, be completely honest.

CHAPTER TEN

Dealing with Creditors

Tim called late one evening. "I know you like to jog early in the morning. Mind if I join you tomorrow? I've just got to talk," he said. I could tell it was urgent by the sound of his voice, so I agreed.

The next morning, we jogged and he talked. "Earlier this week we received three calls from a collection agency representing one of our credit card companies. Cindy talked with them. They were downright mean. They threatened us. We also received two past-due letters from a couple of our creditors. Cindy's scared. What should we do?"

My groan was only partly due to the steep hill we were climbing, but also I felt badly for Tim and Cindy. "Have you been communicating with these lenders? Do they know your situation?" I asked.

"No," Tim responded with surprise. "I haven't made any effort to let them know what's happening. I guess I've tried to avoid them."

Without knowing it, Tim and Cindy were making a common

but dangerous mistake: avoiding communication with their creditors. Most people who get deep in debt develop an attitude that says, "If I ignore the problem, it will eventually go away." But the problem will not go away; in fact, it will intensify. Most creditors are very open to hearing from you, open-minded about your situation, and at times, willing to work out some arrangement for you to repay. The key is good communication and dealing honestly and faithfully with each lender.

DEALING WITH CREDITORS

There are three simple rules to follow when dealing with creditors.

1. Communicate, communicate, communicate.

It is best to run *toward* your creditors, not *away* from them. As hard and as embarrassing as it may be, always take the initiative in keeping your lenders informed. It is almost impossible to negotiate with a creditor you have ignored. Communicating with a creditor sooner rather than later tells them you are responsible and serious about resolving the problem. They document each contact you make with them, whether it is by phone, letter, e-mail, or fax.

The more you communicate, the better. Silence is deadly.

2. Offer lenders a written plan.

Most creditors respond best to a specific request that is backed by a written copy of your budget, a list of your debts, and your proposed repayment plan indicating how much you are able to pay each month. It is important to present a realistic plan, yet to demonstrate you are willing to make sacrifices to pay the debt.

I recommend a cover letter similar to the one below when first communicating with a creditor. You can tailor it to each lender, but putting something in writing is the key.

Dear Sir or Madam:

I am writing to you about my account _____. I am sorry that I have failed to abide by the terms of our agreement. I am committed to full repayment of my debt.

Attached you will find my current budget and a list of my debts. As you can see, my debt totals $_____ and my monthly payments $_____.

My present monthly income of $_____ less my taxes and expenses leaves me only $_____ to pay toward my debts.

I have received assistance in assessing my financial situation to determine what I can afford to pay my creditors at this time.

Enclosed please find my check for $_____. I will be able to pay this each month for the next ____ months. After that time, I will review my finances and may be able to increase my payments.

Also, I respectfully request that the interest rate you are charging be reduced so a greater portion of my payment may go toward principal reduction.

If you are unwilling to accept my proposal, please return the enclosed payment. Contact me at _____, if you have any questions.

Thank you in advance for your help in this matter.

Sincerely,

3. Exercise integrity.

When you communicate with your lenders, always be completely honest. The Bible repeatedly stresses the importance of honesty. Leviticus 19:11 (NASB) says, *"You shall not steal, nor deal falsely, nor lie to one another."* Proverbs states, *"The Lord loathes all cheating and dishonesty"* (20:23 TLB).

Remember, the Lord loves and cares for you. He wants the best for you. Your honesty gives the Lord maximum freedom to work on your behalf.

DEBT MANAGEMENT COMPANIES

One option for helping you work out a repayment plan is to use a debt management company that will represent you to negotiate lower monthly payments and lower interest rates with major credit card companies and certain other creditors. Additional benefits are that you make one monthly payment rather than many, and you stop additional late fees and new over-the-credit-limit fees.

There are several possible downsides to using a debt management company. Some creditors may frown on you working with a debt manager. Other creditors look favorably on the idea. Even so, it is better to use one than forcing creditors to write off your debts or declaring bankruptcy.

Unfortunately, there are many unscrupulous organizations in the business of debt negotiations. You must be very careful to do your homework and deal only with reputable companies. Interview the companies you are considering and compare charges. One of the very best is Financial Hope. Visit their Web site at www.financialhope.com to learn more. And as always, make your decision a matter of prayer before the Lord. You want His wisdom and assistance in choosing the best possible option for you and your situation.

SETTLEMENT COMPANIES AND DEBT NEGOTIATORS

The ads are so tempting. "We can cut your bills in half. If you work with us, you'll pay just pennies on the dollar." It's likely you've seen them on television or heard them on the radio.

Settlement companies (debt negotiators) promise to lower your payoff amounts—dramatically—if you'll let them have your business. That is what they tell you. This is what they don't tell you.

1. *They're going to charge really big fees.* Some companies charge hefty up-front fees, others charge fees based on the amount of debt you owe or the number of your accounts, and some have hidden fees you'll never know about until it's all over. Many also want a piece of the action—a percentage of what the debt creditors agree to wipe away. All together, they usually demand a fee equaling between 20 and 35 percent of your debt. That's big money!

2. *You will have a trashed credit rating.* Settlement companies tell you to stop talking with your creditors and stop making payments. After several months, your creditors will begin writing off your debt. That is when the settlement companies begin talking to your creditors. This process eventually ruins your credit. Write-offs can be the biggest negative factor on your credit report because it means the lender lost money doing business with you. Write-offs will remain on your report for seven years.

3. *Uncle Sam will want his share.* As if sky-high fees and trashed credit were not bad enough, you may also owe federal income taxes on any debt that gets wiped away. That is important for you to understand. When a lender writes off your debt, the amount written off is considered taxable. The lender

may send you an IRS form 1099 that you must file with your federal tax return.

4. *You are being dishonest.* Examine the original loan agreement with your lenders. You have promised in good faith to repay them *fully*. It is one thing if circumstances make it impossible for you to repay, but it is quite another thing to withhold payment and force your creditors to accept less. Essentially, *you* are defrauding them.

Speaking of dishonesty, be wary if a settlement company asks that you send the monthly payments to *them* instead of to your creditors. They hold the money in an account until they agree on a settlement with the credit card company. Unfortunately, that's precisely how many scam artists steal your money. Before you realize the scam, they're long gone with the cash.

Psalm 37:21 tells us that, *"The wicked borrow and do not repay, but the righteous give generously."* Making every effort to repay your lenders keeps you in good standing and honors the Lord in the process.

HOW LENDERS MUST DEAL WITH YOU

The Fair Debt Collection Practices Act protects consumers from abusive practices by debt collectors. Under this law debt collectors have certain rights and certain prohibitions.

What a Debt Collector May Do

Collectors may contact you in person, by telephone, mail, or fax. However, they may not contact you at an inconvenient place or time, such as before 8:00 a.m. or after 9:00 p.m., unless you agree to those terms. Your place of work is also off-limits if the collector knows your employer disapproves.

What a Debt Collector Must Do . . . And Must Not Do

Within five days after you are first contacted, the collector must send you written notice naming the creditor, the amount owed, and what action to take if you believe you do not owe the debt. Make sure you are opening your mail every day to avoid missing an important piece of correspondence from a debt collector.

There are limits on what a debt collector can do. Collectors are prohibited from harassing you. They may not repeatedly call your home or workplace to annoy you. Collectors may not lie or use misleading statements such as misrepresenting the amount you owe or threatening to arrest you. They cannot intimidate you by stating that they will seize your property or garnish your wages unless they intend to take those actions. Any act of intimidation or harassment is prohibited under the Fair Debt Collection Practices Act.

What You Can Do

Report any problem with a debt collector to your state attorney general's office. If you have a question about your rights under the Fair Debt Collection Practices Act, the Federal Trade Commission may be able to assist you. For more information visit www.ftc.gov or seek out someone you know and trust who can point you in the right direction.

TAKING STOCK

In this chapter we've been in the nitty-gritty world of creditors and laws of debt repayment and collection. But the more information you arm yourself with, the better your ability to negotiate and communicate with your lenders with integrity. God cares deeply about you and your reputation with other people. So being completely honest and trustworthy will go a long way in finding favor with the Lord and with those with whom you need to deal.

Make a commitment now to yourself and to the Lord to deal honestly and consistently with everyone in the process. Here's a simple commitment you can make:

I promise to be completely honest and faithful from this point on in all my financial dealings. I make this commitment to the Lord today.

Today's date:_____

Signature:_____

People spend about *one-third more* when they use credit cards rather than cash. Credit card spending seems so painless, not like parting with *real* money.

CHAPTER ELEVEN

Plastic **Surgery**

O ne of the biggest areas of conflict between Tim and Cindy
Connor was their use of plastic—credit cards. They carried
five cards between them, had maxed out two of them, and
were using cash advances from some of the cards to satisfy
the minimum monthly payments on others.

When a statement arrived, it signaled the beginning of an
emotional verbal war between them.

Unfortunately, that's an all-too-common experience among
couples struggling under debt. The easy availability of credit has spawned
a phenomenal growth in the number of cards held by customers.
According to a CNBC survey, the average cardholder has more than
six credit cards, and the average household has more than $8,000 in
credit card debt.

Part of the reason for the explosion in credit cards is the number of solicitations. There are now *billions* of credit card solicitations

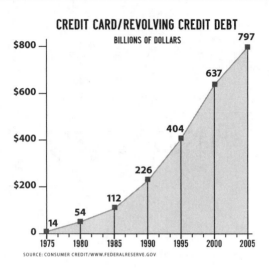

CREDIT CARD/REVOLVING CREDIT DEBT
BILLIONS OF DOLLARS

SOURCE: CONSUMER CREDIT/WWW.FEDERALRESERVE.GOV

each year. Sometimes when I used to open my mailbox, it seemed as if we were receiving half of them!

Even worse, companies continue to solicit younger and younger people—from college students a few years ago to high school students today. And there is only one reason they want your business: *They make lots of money.*

THE BIG MONEY MACHINE

Regardless of what they tell you in their sales pitch, their offer doesn't come because you deserve it, or they like you, or they want to enable you to buy what you want when you want it. They keep tempting you with offers because they make so much money charging exorbitant interest rates. Their profit depends on just one thing—your debt.

That's why they keep raising your credit card limits enticing you to charge more: The more you charge, the more you owe; and the more you owe, the more interest they receive and the more profit they make. It's a big money machine!

How Much Do They Make?

Assume you have $5,560 in credit card debt at an 18 percent interest rate. This would cost you about $1,000 in interest annually. Study the chart below:

Amount of interest you paid:

Year 5	Year 10	Year 20	Year 30	Year 40
$5,000	$10,000	$20,000	$30,000	$40,000

How much the lender earns at 18 percent from your interest payment:

Year 5	Year 10	Year 20	Year 30	Year 40
$7,154	$23,521	$146,628	$790,948	$4,163,213

You can now understand what lenders have understood for a long time—the incredible power of compounding interest. The lender will accumulate a total of $4,163,213 if you pay him $1,000 in interest a year for forty years, and he receives 18 percent on your payments! Is there any wonder credit card companies are eager for you to become one of their borrowers? The key is get yourself in a position where the power of compound interest works *for* you, not *against* you.

How Much You Could Make

The following chart shows what you would accumulate on that same $1,000 if you invested those dollars annually, earning 10 percent:

Year 5	Year 10	Year 20	Year 30	Year 40
$6,453	$17,070	$68,280	$188,373	$527,005

Compare the $40,000 you paid in interest over forty years with the $527,005 you could have accumulated, earning 10 percent on $1,000 each year. The monthly income you could receive from $527,005 is $4,392 if it's earning 10 percent—and you'd never have to touch the principal.

When people take on credit card debt of $5,560 and pay $1,000 a year in interest, the $1,000 in payment—which could have been invested each year and earn 10 percent—has actually cost them $527,005 over forty years. Debt has a much higher cost than many people realize. Next time you are tempted to purchase something with debt, ask yourself if the long-term benefits of staying out of debt outweigh the short-term benefits of the purchase.

Credit card companies also know that people spend about *one-third more* when they use credit cards rather than cash. Credit card spending seems so painless, not like parting with *real* money. As one shopper said to another, "I like credit cards lots more than money because they go so much further—they're just plastic!"

On top of that, only about 43 percent of consumers pay off their entire credit card bills each month. Those who do, use plastic only for convenience or for emergencies. Interestingly, the credit card industry refers to those prudent consumers as "deadbeats." How times have changed. That term used to be reserved for those who *didn't* pay.

Approximately thirty-five million Americans pay only the required minimum—some as low as 2 percent of their balance each month. Many cardholders don't understand the financial consequences of paying only the minimum amount. No matter how good a deal they got on their purchase, how good does it feel twenty years later when they finally pay off their $10,000 debt? If they pay only the monthly minimum at 18 percent interest, that's exactly how long it takes. And instead of $10,000, they will have paid thousands more.

Hopefully by now you're beginning to see the danger of ignoring your credit card problem. If you truly wish to achieve the goal of true financial freedom, then some serious plastic surgery is in order. And in fact, paying off your credit card debt is a key destination on the journey to freedom.

MONEY MAP DESTINATION TWO—PAY OFF CREDIT CARD DEBT

After saving $1,000 for emergencies, the next destination on the road to true financial freedom is paying off all your credit card debt. That's important because of the high interest rates charged by credit cards, usually much higher than other kinds of debt. Here are some proven suggestions for paying off credit cards.

1. Snowball the credit cards.

As we discussed earlier, snowball the cards. Make the largest possible extra payments on the lowest balance card first, paying it off as quickly as possible. Then, add what you were paying on that one to your normal payment on the second lowest balance card until it is paid in full. Repeat the process until they all are paid.

2. Perform plastic surgery.

When I analyze the financial situations of people in debt, I use a simple rule of thumb to determine whether credit cards are too dangerous for them to continue to use. If they do not pay the entire balance at the end of each month, they need to perform plastic surgery—any good pair of scissors will do. Or if they enjoy cooking, they can preheat the oven to 450 degrees and bake the cards until they're golden brown!

3. Limit the cards.

When Bev and I began learning what God says about debt, we had nine credit cards. Today we carry two, and we make certain we pay each balance in full each month. We discovered that we don't need more than one or two cards. It is simpler to monitor them, and it helps us control our spending. And if you pay your bills by check, you have fewer checks to write.

One way to limit the temptations of additional cards (and to make mealtime more peaceful!) is to opt out of receiving telemarketing calls and preapproved credit card offers by mail. Log on the Web site of the National Do Not Call Registry at www.ftc.gov/donotcall to stop telemarketers. To stop junk mail, call toll-free 1-(888)-5OPT-OUT. You'll be really glad you did.

4. Transfer balances to another credit card.

If you carry credit card balances at high interest rates, consider transferring the balance to a card that charges *less* interest. That can save a lot of money. But before transferring to a lower-rate card, confirm that the new card has no transfer fee, no annual fee, and that the interest rate on transferred balances is not higher than the advertised rate; sometimes the low rate offer is only for purchases. And remember, if you miss a payment or make a payment late, you typically forfeit the attractive interest rate. Your interest rate will automatically skyrocket in most cases.

STRATEGIES FOR USING CREDIT CARDS

Selecting the Best Credit Cards

About 6,000 financial institutions issue credit cards and compete for your business. If you have a good credit history, you will be able to choose among them. However, if you are reestablishing your credit history, you will have fewer options.

Here are the key factors to help you choose the best credit card for you:

1. *Interest rate.* Issuers make most of their profit by charging interest. Unbelievably, the top ten card issues earn more than *$25 billion* a year on interest. Make certain you are choosing a card with a good competitive rate.

2. *Annual fees.* Many credit card companies charge an annual fee that ranges from as little as $15 to as much as $395 for a platinum card. The companies justify these fees by the additional services they offer. Beware of hidden and expensive annual fees.

3. *Incentive cards.* As an incentive to use their credit cards, some companies offer frequent flyer mileage, store rebates, or even a percentage of purchases credited toward paying off your mortgage or funding college education. Caution: When using one of these cards, be careful not to purchase things you don't really need just to pile up the mileage or rebates. This subtle temptation requires discipline to keep in check.

Visit www.crownfreeandclear.org for current Web sites that will help you choose the credit cards with the lowest interest rates and fees and the most helpful incentives for you.

Being Diligent

In order to use credit cards wisely, I want to suggest you be diligent to do three things:

1. *Review your statement carefully.* When you receive your credit card statement, review every charge carefully. Surprisingly, most consumers do not. Confirming that every charge is yours will help you detect identity theft more quickly. File

every credit card receipt (not just statements) so you will have evidence in case of a disagreement over a purchase.

2. *Monitor teaser rates.* How many credit card offers have you received that promise unbelievably low rates? These teaser rates are good for a defined period, from a few months to a year. As attractive as they are, the problem is that some cardholders don't switch cards once the teaser rate expires. When it does, the cardholder may be shocked to see the interest due on the next payment because of a very high follow-up rate. Keep an eye on the low rate expiration date, and switch ahead of it.

3. *Check the interest rate on every statement.* Even if you make your credit card payments on time, the card issuer can raise your interest rates automatically if you are late on payments elsewhere—or even if they simply feel you have taken on too much debt. That practice, called the "universal clause," is standard in many credit card agreements. Credit card issuing banks can now easily monitor your credit score.

Using Secured Credit Cards

One of the most effective ways to earn a healthy credit score when you're first starting out or trying to rebuild your credit is to use a secured credit card. You deposit a sum of money in a bank, and that amount becomes your credit limit. For example, if you deposited $500, then $500 will be your credit limit. You cannot withdraw your deposit as long as you are using the credit card. The bank takes no risk because if you don't pay your outstanding balance each month, they simply deduct it from your deposit.

TAKING STOCK

Before going any further, I want to urge you to spend some time reflecting on your current use of credit cards. Because of their ease of use and almost unlimited availability, credit card debt can sneak up on you and cause more heartache and financial damage than you can imagine. It is important that you be honest with yourself and with the Lord on this issue.

If you reach Destination Two successfully, with the Lord's gracious help, you will be well on your way to achieving true financial freedom. So please implement the suggestions in this chapter. You'll be so glad you did.

Car debt is one of the biggest roadblocks for most people on their journey to true financial freedom. Most people never get out of it.

CHAPTER TWELVE

The Auto Debt Trap

The next time I met with the Connors, Tim had a confession to make. "The reason I bought the expensive sports car was my pride. I wanted to look successful in the eyes of my neighbors and people at work."

The Connors were paying a high price for Tim's need to look prosperous—$350 a month for six years! Not only was it undermining their budget, that shiny little car had lost so much value that after four years of those high payments, he still owed $5,000 more than it was worth. That's a common problem many people face.

After home mortgages, car loans are the largest debts most people carry. And most people have them. More than 70 percent of all the cars purchased in this country are bought with borrowed money. Someone once joked that the only reason banks have drive-in windows is so the cars can see their owners!

The last time Bev and I purchased a car, the salesperson started to discuss how we were going to pay for it. He almost went into shock when we said, "We'll pay cash." And many auto sellers discourage paying by cash because of the potential loss in revenue if you were to finance through their finance companies. So beware.

THE HARD TRUTH

Let me be blunt. *Car debt is one of the biggest roadblocks for most people on their journey to true financial freedom.* It is especially dangerous because most people never get out of it. Just when they get to the point of paying off a car, dazzled by the thoughts of a newer model, they trade it in and purchase that newer one with credit.

Unlike a home, which usually appreciates in value, the moment you drive a car off the lot it *depreciates,* or decreases in value. It's worth less than you paid for it by the time you hit the first intersection. You've probably heard the expression, "upside down on a car loan." The meaning is simple: You owe more for the car than it is worth. If you had to sell it, you couldn't get enough to pay off the loan.

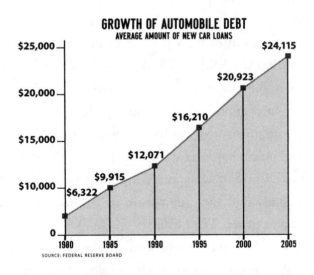

GROWTH OF AUTOMOBILE DEBT
AVERAGE AMOUNT OF NEW CAR LOANS

SOURCE: FEDERAL RESERVE BOARD

THE AUTO DEBT TRAP

There are several reasons that so many of us have been trapped by auto debt. First, the cost of a car has become increasingly expensive. I'm old enough to remember paying $2,000 for a brand-new car. That's about what a set of upgraded rims and a sound system cost today!

Second, advertisers have done a masterful job of marketing an expensive image rather than selling a car as affordable, reliable transportation. Their ads promise status and sex appeal that lead to an exciting, carefree life. All of that becomes yours—the moment you buy their car!

NOTHING DEPRECIATES A CAR FASTER THAN HAVING YOUR NEIGHBOR BUY A NEW ONE.

© Marc Shaw. Used by permission.

Third, the cost of financing has risen significantly. As cars have become more expensive, lenders have gone to providing longer loans. Not long ago, three years was the maximum. Today, loans can go up to seven years for a brand-new vehicle. One car dealer I know explained the reason: "Customers don't ask about the price anymore. They just want to know if they can afford the monthly payments. And most of them don't care how long they have to make them."

Thankfully, there is a way out of this trap if you're willing to take it.

ESCAPING THE AUTO DEBT TRAP

By now you know that getting into financial trouble is often much easier than getting out. But I know from experience that a systematic plan and a strong resolve to climbing out of the trap will work. Let me offer you four steps to get out of auto debt.

1. Decide to keep your car at least three years longer than your car loan.
2. Pay off your car loan. Use the snowball principles discussed in chapter 10 to eliminate your auto loan. Be systematic and aggressive in applying as many dollars as possible to paying off that loan.
3. After your last payment, keep making the payment, but pay it to *yourself.* Put it into an account that you'll use to buy your next car.
4. Buy your next car with cash. When you're ready to replace your car, the saved cash plus the trade-in value should be sufficient to buy a car without credit. It may not be a new car, but you should be able to buy a low-mileage used car without any debt.

LEANING AGAINST CULTURE

When Bev and I first learned God's financial principles, we realized that if we were going to experience true financial freedom, we would need to get out of car debt—for good! So we made several key decisions.

We chose to buy used cars rather than new ones, avoiding the worst depreciation loss any car experiences—the first day off the lot. Then, *we decided to keep them as long as they were safe to drive.* Many people itch to buy another car as soon as the new car smell fades or as soon as their car starts needing repairs. But as Crown's cofounder, Larry Burkett, used to say, "The cheapest car to drive is usually the one you already own."

We also realized it would be smart to limit the use of our cars because of the cost of driving. A Hertz Rental Car survey found that the average cost of driving a new car, including gas, maintenance, depreciation, and standard repairs, is $.57 a mile. If we could reduce driving by ten miles a day, it would save $5.70 a day or $2,080 a year. That represents significant savings.

Because these decisions were so countercultural, we knew we would feel pressure to buy new or trade up, so we felt it would be important to have a good sense of humor concerning our cars. So we laughed at the cars and ourselves . . . all the way to the bank.

Bev's car was a low-mileage used car that she drove for seventeen years! The last few years she drove it, we called it "Puff," because a little puff of smoke emerged from the tailpipe anytime she accelerated.

During those seventeen years, I drove two cars. The first was a truck that cost $100. A neighbor once borrowed it and had it painted, which made it look like a $200 truck. But I really enjoyed driving that old truck and never got stressed out if it got dinged. I could haul anything and not be worried about damaging it, and it got great gas mileage. Insurance was cheap. And after driving it for several years, I sold it for $700. It's the only vehicle I've ever sold for a profit!

My children nicknamed the second car "Chiquita." Well, they actually called it the "Rotten Chiquita" because the brownish-yellow color reminded them of an overripe banana. It was so ugly that the children in the neighborhood once stopped in the middle of an intense basketball game to laugh at it as I drove past them.

Yet I remember driving the Chiquita to work early one morning while having a very special time with the Lord. And a Bible passage came to mind : *"In Your presence is fullness of joy"* (Psalm 16:11 NASB). I realized it didn't matter whether I was driving the most expensive car made or that old Chiquita. True joy comes from knowing the Lord well, not by what we drive.

Then I began to wonder: What would the incredibly rich King Solomon have paid for the Chiquita? It could go sixty miles an hour, had air-conditioning and a radio. I think he would have paid a fortune. But in our culture, if it's not the latest and greatest, it's just not appreciated. So I want to challenge you. When you are deciding which car to buy, do not allow the expectations of our culture to compel you to spend more than you should for your vehicle.

Here are a couple of other matters you need to consider related to automobile debt.

OTHER CAUTIONS ABOUT AUTO DEBT

About Auto Dealer Financing

If you do choose to obtain an auto loan, you have options. When you finance a car through a dealership, the dealer normally asks several lenders to bid on your loan. Based on your credit, the lenders give the dealer a "buy rate"—the interest rate the lenders will accept.

The dealer, however, usually doesn't offer you the buy rate offered by the lenders. Instead, he quotes a higher rate called the *dealer markup*. The dealer either pockets the markup or splits it with the lender.

Never assume that the rate you get from the dealership, or a financing company related to a dealership, is the best rate you can receive.

Let me offer a suggestion: After you have negotiated the price on the car, ask the dealer to propose the best financing deal. After you receive the dealership's financing offer, check with your own bank or credit union for a comparative offer. Many times savvy buyers can improve on the dealer's interest rate—and save hundreds of dollars. Avoid accepting the first option offered to you. Typically, there are better deals to be had.

Automobile Leasing—Just Another Name for Debt

Leasing has become a popular alternative to buying a car. Car companies usually lease about 20 percent of their new cars. The attraction for consumers is that lease payments are usually lower than purchase payments, and so it looks like you're getting more for less.

But there are some huge downsides to leasing. At the end of a purchase loan, you own the car, but at the end of a lease, you own *nothing*. In addition to returning the car to the dealer, you might be charged for excessive mileage. Most leasing agreements limit you to 12,000 miles per year. At $.20 for each additional mile, many people face a final bill of several thousand dollars.

It also can be very expensive, if not impossible, to get out of a car lease early. Life can take sudden turns and what you think you can afford one year may be an impossible burden the next. Being strapped to a lease agreement will only add to your financial woes.

An auto lease agreement is just another name for debt, so I suggest you avoid that trap too.

Repossession

If you find yourself in a real financial bind and are unable to make your auto payments, you really only have two options. You can attempt to sell the car yourself for at least the payoff amount or have the lender repossess it. And I strongly suggest you do everything you can to avoid repossession. When a lender recovers a vehicle by repossession, normally he sells it at an auction receiving only a rock-bottom price. Then, the lender can sue you for the deficiency and your credit score is destroyed.

Here are a couple of steps to help you avoid this potentially long-term setback.

1. Meet with a lender. Seek an agreement with a lender to loan you the money for the difference between the sales price and the amount you owe.
2. Sell the car yourself. Take pains to clean it up as much as possible. Purchase some new floor mats and do some minor repairs. All these little things add up to you getting closer to a top-dollar sale.

By selling the car yourself and avoiding repossession, you protect your credit score and honor the Lord by not violating your agreement with the creditor.

A PARTING THOUGHT FROM A WISE CONSUMER—MY WIFE!

At first, I (Bev) was not excited about the idea of buying used cars and then driving them until the wheels were ready to fall off. But when I understood that this would save us so much in interest and depreciation—money that we could use to pay off the rest of our debts—I was ready to try it. Sure, there were times when I wanted another car, but reaching the goal of becoming debt-free became more important to me than driving a newer, more expensive car. I'm so glad Howard and I made the hard decisions and stuck with commitments we made. And I'm convinced you will be glad you did as well.

I'd encourage you to pay off your cars and stay out of auto debt. It's a major step in reaching your goal of true financial freedom.

TAKING STOCK

1. Assessing your emotions: Where are you emotionally on the issue of car debt? (circle one)

   Frustrated   *Indifferent*   *Confused*   *Excited About Getting Out!*

2. In the space below, list what you believe are your next steps in addressing your current auto debt . . . how you will begin to eliminate it. Use as many steps as you feel you need.

   Step 1

   Step 2

   Step 3

   Step 4

3. Truth reminder:

   "The borrower is servant to the lender." (Proverbs 22:7)

Paying for a college education presents a great opportunity for parents and teenagers to grow closer together as a family and with the Lord.

CHAPTER THIRTEEN

School Days, School Days, Dear Old Loans and Debt Days

During one of our conversations with Tim and Cindy, Tim mentioned his younger sister, Jean, and her husband, Mark.

Mark and Jean Dixon were high school sweethearts who shared a common dream for their careers—they wanted to become teachers. They enrolled in the same university and majored in education. They married during their senior year.

Mark and Jean graduated from college and left for their first teaching jobs with all their earthly possessions in their small car—along with $55,000 in school loans, $4,500 in credit card debt, and a car loan.

The Dixons began their teaching careers with high hopes and a commitment to influence their students for the Lord. They weren't prepared for the difficulty of making ends meet on teachers' starting salaries. Then six months later, the school loan payments began. They panicked as the difficult became impossible. Not knowing what else to do, they used credit cards to make the payments, creating new debts to service the old.

Their dream had become a nightmare. Even though they loved teaching, they began to consider changing careers in order to earn more money. Their mounting frustration over debt diminished their effectiveness in the classroom, intensified the stress at home, and brought a dark cloud over their life. I can't tell you how many times I've seen this over the years. So many people struggle under the relentless weight of school loans.

A GROWING DILEMMA

Millions of college graduates face a challenge similar to that of Tim's sister and her husband. School debt forces many into jobs or locations they would not otherwise have chosen. It also pressures some young couples to postpone marriage or beginning a family. And some who have felt the Lord calling them into full-time ministry have not been able to pursue it because they could not afford it.

Ron Blue, an outstanding financial advisor and author, tells of a young man who wanted to go to seminary to become a missionary. The young man had no money and thought a student loan was his only possible way to pay for it. But by the time he graduated, he would be responsible for a $40,000 debt. How would he pay that back on a missionary's budget?

After much prayer, he decided to enroll without the help of a student loan, trusting the Lord to meet his needs. God responded in some remarkable ways to this young man's faith. The young, grateful student graduated without borrowing anything and grew in his appreciation for how the living God could provide his needs. That turned out to be his most valuable seminary lesson as he prepared for life on the mission field. Stated simply: Borrowing often denies God an opportunity to demonstrate His faithfulness.

Unfortunately, school loans incurred by college students represent one of the fastest growing areas of debt. *USA Today* recently asked college students, "What are you most fearful of at this time?" Nearly one-third, 32 percent, answered, "Going deeply into debt." That should not have to be one of the biggest challenges they face.

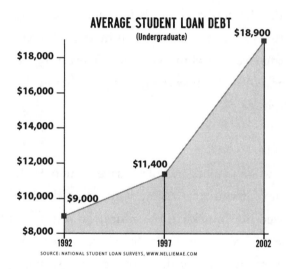

AVERAGE STUDENT LOAN DEBT
(Undergraduate)

SOURCE: NATIONAL STUDENT LOAN SURVEYS, WWW.NELLIEMAE.COM

Consider these statistics:

- The average graduating senior has $3,300 in credit card debt and about $19,000 in school loans.
- Students who finish graduate school owe an average of $39,000 in school loans.
- Bankruptcies among eighteen- to twenty-four-year-olds have doubled in the last ten years.

LIMITING SCHOOL DEBT

Your objective is to graduate (or help your children to graduate) from college with little or no school debt so that you will be free to follow the Lord. Here are ways to help you limit or even avoid college debt.

Recognize that paying for a college education presents a great opportunity for parents and teenagers to grow closer together as a family and with the Lord. My advice is as soon as your child is old enough, schedule a regular time to meet together and pray for the Lord to provide the necessary funds for their future education. Ask God for creative solutions that will eliminate or reduce the need to borrow. And then wait for Him to respond. The Lord is eager to reveal Himself to each of us by answering our prayers and demonstrating His awesome power.

What Parents Can Do

It is a blessing when parents are able to save to help pay for their children's education. If you start saving while your children are young, you'll be amazed how quickly those education reserves will accumulate with time and consistency. The key is to *consistently* save, even a small amount, month by month. Here are some saving options that you might consider:

- State-sponsored 529 plans
- State-sponsored Prepaid Tuition Plan
- Coverdell Educational Savings Account
- Roth individual retirement account

Each of these options has strengths and limitations. Visit www.crownfreeandclear.org for a current explanation of each or see a reliable and well-respected financial planner in your area. Regardless of which you choose, the earlier you can begin to save, the better. Time is your friend because your savings grows through compounding interest.

What Children Can Do

Many parents and grandparents are not in a financial position to fund all or even part of their child's education. If you're one of them—don't feel guilty! You can only do what you can do, and this may be a blessing in disguise.

When they are old enough, *the first way your children can help is to begin working* to save for their college—and the sooner, the better. They may work part- or full-time during summer vacation and perhaps part-time during the school year. Be careful to maintain a good balance between having your children participate in saving for college and allowing them the freedom to enjoy their teenage years. When they enter college, encourage them to work part-time, and consider seeking a summer job. When students work to help pay for college, they appreciate the experience more and are more serious about their studies.

Some of the most mature and responsible young adults I know worked their way through college. Crown's cofounder, Larry Burkett, did—taking six years instead of four—and an added benefit was the way it built his character and work ethic.

My parents paid for my tuition, and I worked for my spending money as a waiter. In retrospect, I see many advantages to my working. Working part-time forced me to learn how to manage my time efficiently, and I spent what I earned more carefully. Also, I learned people skills. Anyone who waits tables receives an education in human nature!

A second way children can help with college expenses is to consider less expensive education options at the beginning. Attending a community college near home for the first two years typically is less expensive than enrolling in a four-year college, especially if it is possible for the student to live at home. The added benefit is the student has an opportunity to explore the college setting and pursue a variety of subjects without the added pressure of huge financial commitments.

A third way your children can help is by exploring available grants and scholarships—not simply leaving that to parents. Many colleges and states offer substantial savings and finding those dollars can be uniquely motivating to the prospective student. Go to www.crownfreeandclear. org for links to Web sites with information on grants and scholarships. Also, I recommend Tom Shaw's excellent book for parents and their teens called *Collegebound* (Moody, 2005). It offers several helpful strategies for finding and stretching tuition dollars. Another fine resource is Gordon Wadsworth's *Cost Effective College* (Moody, 2000), which includes tips for completing scholarship applications and essays and locating public and private scholarships.

Finally, if your child is considering service in the military, *remember that all branches offer educational benefits.* Be sure that he fully understands the obligations and what is being offered before making any commitment. Also be sure to ask for a letter that confirms the military's educational obligations so that there are no questions in the future.

PAYING OFF SCHOOL DEBT

Still, even after all these options are considered, many students end up graduating from college with sizeable debt. The need for a repayment strategy is critical.

Where can someone with student loans go for help? For people who have more than one school loan, loan consolidation options may be your best place to turn. It can reduce your interest rate and lower your monthly payment.

Basically, there are two types of school loan lenders: the government and private companies. The government usually offers the lowest interest rates because they want to encourage people to go to college. That's why the government subsidizes the loans in order to drive down cost.

The government has established an excellent Web site that will allow you to apply for student loan consolidation directly over the Internet. Check out www.loanconsolidation.ed.gov for more information.

There are three factors that influence your interest rate and whether you may consolidate school loans:

- The current interest rates charged for school loans.
- The current interest rates you are paying on your loans. The lower your current rates, the lower the consolidated rate they will offer.
- The government will allow you to consolidate only once.

Even if you can't consolidate your school loans, establish the goal of paying them off as soon as possible by putting in place some of the debt reduction strategies we've already discussed in previous chapters.

Whether you are planning to pay for college or facing a significant college debt burden, you need to develop a plan. Being deliberate and then committing your plan to the Lord will get you off on the right road toward more and more freedom. Remember: The goal is to be free and clear of all debt. Eliminating your college debt will help you reach that goal.

TAKING STOCK

1. A few chapters back in chapter 7 we looked at the power of changing your mind-set in order to think the way God thinks about finances and debts. Take some time to consider what the Lord would have you to do in regard to either (a) planning to minimize or eliminate the need for using debt for college or (b) paying off your school loans. Then prayerfully seek His guidance.

2. Write down some available resources to you:

   Scholarships and grants . . .

   Employment opportunities . . .

   Parents' or grandparents' gifts or support . . .

We did not start prepaying the home mortgage until we eradicated all our credit card and consumer debt. Then we focused on the home.

CHAPTER FOURTEEN

Paying Off
Your Mortgage

The message light on the phone was blinking when I arrived home after a long and demanding trip. Exhausted, I pushed the button.

"Hello, Howard. This is Tim Connor." I hadn't heard from him in some time, and I was curious to know how things were going. "Cindy and I are doing really well, but we have quite a disagreement over whether we should try to pay off our home mortgage. Could we talk this over with you?"

I returned his call and we set an appointment for three days later. It was great to hear that they had made solid progress by paying off their credit card and consumer debts. Now Cindy felt they should try to pay off their home mortgage, but Tim was reluctant. He said defensively, "I don't want us to lose the tax advantage of the mortgage payment. Our interest each year is one of our biggest tax deductions. What do you think?"

I explained, "The tax advantage is often misunderstood and

overrated. You are in the 25 percent tax bracket, so for each $1,000 you pay in home mortgage interest, you save $250 in taxes—25 percent of the $1,000 interest paid. You still paid $750 in taxes. So while there is a tax benefit, it's not as much as you may think. Paying $1,000 to save $250 is not *that* great a deal."

"Well," Tim interrupted, "I'd also rather invest the money and earn a greater return than the interest we pay on our mortgage."

"Sure," I responded. "That makes a lot of sense. There's just one catch—there's no such thing as a sure thing in investing. Here's my advice: *Do both.* Allocate some of your monthly surplus to investing and some to accelerating the payment of your mortgage."

Tim nodded his head. "That sounds like a reasonable approach." And Cindy agreed.

THE MORTGAGE QUESTION

When Bev and I first learned God's financial principles as a young married couple, we began to ask ourselves what the Lord wanted for us concerning debt. Should we pay off our mortgage too? We became convinced that the Lord wanted us entirely out of debt, even our home mortgage. We understood this to be a *really* long-term goal because of the size of our mortgage and our other debts. But we also knew that Proverbs 21:5 says, *"Steady plodding brings prosperity"* (TLB). So we committed to be "steady plodders" and trust God to multiply our efforts.

Bev and I realized that if we could pay off our home mortgage, our cost of living would be much lower. It was our largest expense. It would free up a significant part of our income so that we could give much more generously to the work of Christ *and* save and invest more aggressively to reach our goal of true financial freedom.

Without a mortgage, we would enjoy greater financial stability as a family. We could better cope with the cost of a serious illness, loss of a job, or other unexpected financial emergencies. And it would allow Bev to do something she really wanted to do: stay at home and raise our young children.

We did not start prepaying the home mortgage until we eradicated all our credit card and consumer debt. Then we focused on the home. But before we could begin to make headway against our mortgage, we needed to understand the numbers involved. And you do too.

UNDERSTANDING THE AMORTIZATION SCHEDULE

Every mortgage comes with a payment schedule, also called an amortization schedule, based on the length of the loan and the interest rate. Knowing how this schedule works will help you develop a sound plan for paying off the mortgage. Let's examine the payment schedule of a mortgage.

Please do not let the mortgage size or the interest rate in this illustration hinder your thinking. This is for illustration purposes only. In the example on the next page, we are assuming a $150,000 mortgage at a 7.5 percent fixed interest rate, paid over thirty years.

As you can see (on page 140), the payments during the first year are largely interest. Of the $12,585.84 in payments, only $1,382.73 went toward principal reduction. In fact, it will be twenty-three years before the principal and interest portions of the payment equal each other!

Now here's something really important to remember. *Interest is charged on the remaining unpaid principal balance.* Look at the schedule on the next page.

Pay #	Month	Payment	Interest	Principal	Balance
0					150,000.00
1	Jan	1,048.82	937.50	111.32	149,888.68
2	Feb	1,048.82	936.80	112.02	149,776.66
3	Mar	1,048.82	936.10	112.72	149,663.94
4	Apr	1,048.82	935.40	113.42	149,550.52
5	May	1,048.82	934.69	114.13	149,436.39
6	Jun	1,048.82	933.98	114.84	149,321.55
7	Jul	1,048.82	933.26	115.56	149,205.98
8	Aug	1,048.82	932.54	116.28	149,089.70
9	Sep	1,048.82	931.81	117.01	148,972.69
10	Oct	1,048.82	931.08	117.74	148,854.95
11	Nov	1,048.82	930.34	118.48	148,736.47
12	Dec	1,048.82	929.60	119.22	148,617.25
Totals:		12,585.84	11,203.11	1,382.73	

In January, if you paid your first monthly payment of $1,048.82 *plus* the next month's principal payment of $112.02, the principal balance would be $149,776.66. So in February when you make your regular payment of $1,048.82, it is applied as though it were payment number 3. Now, look carefully at payment 2. You paid $112.02 extra and saved the $936.80 in interest you would have paid. That is a great deal! Can you see why I hope that you will catch the vision of paying off your home?

You can visit www.crownfreeandclear.org and click on "Tools" for a mortgage calculator, which will help you determine how much you can shorten your mortgage and save more than you might think by making extra payments of various amounts. There's nothing magical about what I'm suggesting. Once you understand how it works, the numbers will begin to work *for* you.

HOW TO PAY OFF THE MORTGAGE MORE QUICKLY

I don't know about you, but a thirty-year goal to pay off my home mortgage doesn't excite me—it seems like forever. But if I can shorten it, the goal is much more attainable. There are several ways to accelerate the payment of your home mortgage.

1. Reduce the length of the mortgage.

If you need a new mortgage or the conditions are favorable for you to refinance, consider a shorter-term mortgage. If you can afford higher payments, go with a 15-year instead of a 30-year mortgage. The interest rate on a 15-year mortgage is normally lower than the 30-year rate, and the outstanding balance shrinks much faster.

Let's compare a $150,000 30-year mortgage at 7.5 percent and a 15-year mortgage at 7 percent.

Total Mortgage $150,000	30 Years	15 Years
Monthly Payment	$1,048	$1,348
At the end of 15 years:		
Interest paid	$151,928	$92,683
Principal paid	$ 36,859	$150,000
Principal balance due	$ 131,140	0 (Yes!)
Interest paid years 15–30	$ 75,649	0
Total interest paid	$ 227,577	$ 92,683

If you can shrink the duration of your mortgage in half and save a half percent on your interest rate, the savings in total interest is huge.

Here's the key question for you to answer: Can I afford the larger monthly payment? If it will put too much strain on your budget or will not allow you to meet your other financial goals, then I recommend a longer mortgage with a lower monthly payment.

2. Add something to the required payment.

You can still accelerate the repayment of your mortgage simply by paying an extra amount each month or as frequently as possible.

That's what Bev and I did. We started small. Each month we put a little more on the mortgage to reduce the principal more quickly. The longer we did it, the more excited we became.

One easy method of prepaying is to set up an automatic withdrawal from your checking account each month. Many banks participate in online banking services as well. This is an easy way to manage and keep track of your monthly payments.

3. Bonuses and tax returns.

Finally, when you receive a work bonus or an income tax refund, give generously to the Lord and then consider applying the rest to your home mortgage. Doing that each time it occurs can have a significant impact on paying off your home.

I remember receiving an unexpected bonus. Instead of taking a vacation or buying something nice but not necessary, Bev and I applied those dollars toward the mortgage. Because the funds went directly against the principal, that bonus alone allowed us to shorten our mortgage by several years!

TIME TO GET PRACTICAL

Once you have decided to pay off your home, you need to take these steps to make certain your mortgage and your lender line up with that plan:

1. Examine your mortgage to confirm that it can be prepaid without penalty. Most mortgages allow this.

2. Let your lender know what you are planning. Not many borrowers prepay their mortgages, so the lender may be in shock for a while!

3. If you pay by check, write one for your regular payment and a separate check for the amount of principal prepaid. That will create a paper trail should there ever be a question of your prepaying history. If you pay electronically, keep a copy of your monthly bank statements.

4. Get a payment schedule (amortization schedule) for your mortgage and track your progress every month. This is very important. You'll be enormously encouraged as you see the balance reducing. Remember, paying off your home mortgage usually takes years, and you'll need lots of encouragement to stay at it.

5. Once a year, contact your lender to confirm the unpaid balance of the mortgage. Do that consistently to make certain the lender is properly crediting your prepayments.

REFINANCING YOUR MORTGAGE

When interest rates drop, it may be wise to consider refinancing your mortgage at a lower interest rate. As a rule of thumb, refinancing makes sense when you can pay for the costs of refinancing within two to three years with the money you save each month from the lower interest rate.

Sadly, many people use the refinance option to increase the amount of house debt and unwisely spend the cash they take out. If you refinance, use this opportunity to reduce the number of years left on your mortgage. For example, if you can reduce its length from thirty years to twenty while still making about the same monthly payment, do it!

FIXED RATE VERSUS ADJUSTABLE RATE MORTGAGES

Interest rates may be fixed or adjustable. A fixed-rate mortgage charges the same rate of interest during the life of the mortgage. The advantage of the fixed rate is that your payment is predictable. There is less risk because rising interest rates will not increase your monthly payment.

An adjustable-rate mortgage, commonly called an ARM, periodically adjusts its rate to reflect the current market. The two advantages of an ARM are that the initial rate is usually lower than a fixed rate, and if rates go down, so does your monthly payment. However, when rates escalate, an ARM can devastate your finances.

Consider an adjustable-rate mortgage if you plan on staying in your home seven years or less *and* the government is trying to help economic growth by reducing interest rates. Otherwise, I recommend a fixed-rate mortgage.

To compare home mortgages and interest rates, visit www.crownfreeandclear.org for links to outstanding Web sites that provide current information. But for our purposes here you need to know there are mortgages that should be avoided and other costly options you need to understand.

MORTGAGES TO AVOID

Biweekly Payments

A biweekly payment means that you pay half of the monthly payment every two weeks. Many consumers receive biweekly payment offers—usually laced with deception. Most of the offers come through third party companies that charge for this service. Making twenty-six biweekly payments a year is simply the equivalent of making thirteen monthly payments instead of twelve. You can make one extra monthly payment a year or add one-twelfth of a payment each month and save the fee! Please take my advice: Don't use a biweekly payment plan to prepay your mortgage.

Interest-Only Mortgages

Interest-only mortgages have become increasingly popular. Because no portion of the payment goes toward principal, the payments are lower and customers are able to qualify for a more expensive house.

They are *very* dangerous. Since there is no reduction of principal, if the home drops in value, the loan balance will be greater than the value of the home. If the rate on the interest-only mortgage is adjustable, then payments can increase—sometimes significantly.

The bottom line: Don't be tempted by interest-only mortgages. They are far too dangerous for most people.

MORTGAGE INSURANCE: WHAT YOU SHOULD KNOW

Many homebuyers do not understand mortgage insurance. If you secure a home loan with less than a 20 percent down payment, your lender probably will require you to buy mortgage insurance (PMI) to protect their interests in case you default.

Mortgage insurance is very expensive. The monthly cost is about $45 for every $100,000 of the original mortgage amount. For example, on a $150,000 mortgage, the monthly cost is about $68.

Once the equity in your home reaches 20 percent, you can stop carrying mortgage insurance unless you have an FHA loan, which requires premium payments to the government for the life of the loan.

The law requires your lender to cancel your mortgage insurance when your loan balance shrinks to 78 percent of the home's originally appraised value. You may request cancellation once it reaches 80 percent.

However, the law allows lenders to require mortgage insurance for "high-risk" borrowers until the balance drops to 50 percent of the home's value. If you have missed payments, you may be considered high-risk.

You can eliminate mortgage insurance sooner if you prepay on the loan and build your equity faster. Also, if your home has appreciated significantly, some lenders will consider a new appraisal instead of the original one when deciding if you've met the 20 percent equity threshold.

TAKING STOCK

Bev Dayton's Two Cents

The idea of owning our home mortgage-free appealed to me. Howard and I knew it wasn't going to happen overnight, and it didn't. But we paid off the mortgage faster than we initially hoped because the Lord provided additional funds for us in an unexpected way.

When we paid the last mortgage payment, I was surprised to feel a wonderful sense of freedom and relief. I realized that if Howard would die before my children went out on their own, I would be able to continue raising them in our home. That was a huge source of comfort.

I believe that the Lord wants us totally free from debt—even our homes. So, if you own a home, I encourage you to seek the Lord on the issue and learn whether He would have you begin paying off the mortgage. If He leads you to do it, He will also provide the way.

Limit your potential loss to the cash you invest and the asset itself. Don't jeopardize your family's needs by risking all your personal assets on investment debt.

CHAPTER FIFTEEN

Investment and Business Debt

A few weeks after meeting with Tim and Cindy to discuss their home mortgage questions, I received an e-mail from Tim. Here's part of it: "We both feel really good about your advice to split our surplus funds between prepaying our mortgage and doing some investing. Last night I saw a TV program about buying rental properties with no money down. A lot of folks are making a pile of money without having to invest anything. Since we don't have much cash to invest yet, I thought this might be a great way to jump-start our investing.

"I'm ready to get the home-study course and take the next step. What do you think?"

Within two seconds I hit the reply button. "Hi, Tim. Good to hear from you. Please don't do anything on this until we have a chance to talk next week."

The next week when we met, I thought Tim might launch into orbit. "I've seen two more of those programs," he said, "and I can't wait to get started. The stories are inspiring. People have made tens of thousands of dollars in only a few weeks. It looks like just the thing we need!"

Sadly, too many people like Tim have fallen prey to get-rich-quick schemes and lived to regret it. I really want you to avoid that mistake.

THE DANGER OF INFOMERCIALS AND GET-RICH-QUICK GIMMICKS

The "free" seminars and relentless flood of television infomercials that promise to teach you how to make a fortune in real estate with no money down neglect to mention two little words: *mortgage debt!*

ED, I'M THIS CLOSE TO PERFECTING A "GET RICH QUICK" PLAN THAT I'VE BEEN WORKING ON FOR THIRTY YEARS.

© Andy Robertson. Used by permission.

They forget to explain that little or no money down translates into higher interest rates and larger mortgage payments. Then what happens when a vacancy comes and you have months without rental income? You still have to keep making payments.

My advice: Don't go to the seminar. And change the channel!

BORROWING MONEY TO INVEST

Let's broaden the question: Should you borrow money to make an investment? In my opinion, it is permissible to borrow for an investment, but only if the investment (along with your down payment) is the sole collateral for the debt. You should not personally guarantee repayment of the debt. At first, this may appear to contradict the biblical admonition for godly people to repay their debts. But let's explore this issue further.

Suppose you wanted to purchase a rental property with a reasonable down payment, making sure that the house would be the sole security for the debt. You would explain to potential lenders that at your option, you would repay the loan in one of two ways: either by giving the lender cash—making the specified payments—or by giving the lender the property plus the down payment and any other money you had invested in the house.

Given those options, the lender must make a decision. Is the down payment sufficient? Is the house of adequate value? Is the real estate market strong enough for the lender to feel secure about making the loan?

Some investors have responded that it is impossible to locate a lender willing to loan without a personal guarantee. However, I have seen the Lord allow people to secure this type of financing. So I know it is possible.

When I was in the real estate development business, I prayed for this type of financing and then knocked on lots of doors. Eventually I got it. Some of the loans came from owners selling their properties, some came from lending institutions. Typically, I would offer 25 percent as the down payment and ask for a mortgage of no longer than fifteen years.

Because of the possibility of difficult financial events over which you have no control, be sure to limit your potential loss to the cash you invest and the asset itself. It is painful to lose your investment, but it is much more serious to jeopardize your family's needs by risking all your personal assets on investment debt. What

I'm suggesting may appear too conservative, but many people have become slaves of the lender and lost everything by guaranteeing debt on investments that went sour.

After explaining these concepts to the Connors, Cindy seemed relieved. Tim, although disappointed, responded, "I guess I should have known that if something seems too good to be true, it probably is. I have to admit that I'm half tempted to try it anyway, but all your advice has helped us so much—I've got to trust you on this one."

Still, there's another type of debt that needs to be evaluated—the debt incurred for starting or growing a business.

WHAT ABOUT BUSINESS DEBT?

The Story of Dewey and Bill

Dewey Kemp and Bill Geary dreamed of owning their own office supply company. For years they saved every penny they could scrape together to get the business off the ground. They also felt the Lord prompting them to make a commitment to do something outside the box—almost unheard of in their industry—grow the business *without* using debt.

Dewey recalls, "When you don't use debt, it forces you to be creative. We knew that our biggest challenge would be to grow the inventory, staff, and accounts receivable just from profits. So we decided to focus on serving only the business community, and we didn't sell to any customers who would not commit to paying their bill in twenty days. We also elected to carry a very limited inventory of high-turnover items, ordering everything else we needed every night from a wholesale company that delivered by five o'clock the next morning. This allowed us to grow without the overhead of expensive inventory or additional warehouse space.

"We were able to offer our customers the best pricing and service in town by setting up a convenient system for them to order from us over the Internet.

"Here's the biggest lesson we learned: The less you have in resources, the more resourceful you have to be. When we ultimately sold our business, the purchaser was amazed that we operated without debt. It gave us a natural opportunity to share how Jesus Christ and His principles shaped our company."

MY RECOMMENDATION FOR YOU

If you are in business, here's my recommendation: *Use as little debt as possible, and pay it off as quickly as possible!*

When you operate with little or no debt, it allows you to compete favorably against companies saddled with lots of debt because you are not burdened with large interest payments. It also provides the business more financial stability to weather unexpected challenges.

Jack Nixon and his brother owned a large car dealership in central Florida. He enrolled in a Crown Financial Ministries small-group study and learned God's perspective on debt. Jack and his brother decided to try eliminating all their business debt. They started by accelerating the mortgage payments on their land and building. After several years, they were mortgage-free.

Their next goal was to pay off all the new cars in inventory, but after three years they had not made much progress. That was a mystery to them since their auto sales were very strong. After hiring a second auditor, they discovered the problem: Their most trusted employee had embezzled more than $2 million. Jim said, "If we had not paid off the land and building, we would not have survived the theft. Thank the Lord for the vision to work toward becoming debt-free."

One of the most common reasons for the failure of start-up businesses is lack of capital. When you begin a business with borrowed money, you invite additional pressure to be profitable quickly. Many businesses require several years to become profitable. Take your time. Save as much as possible before launching your business. The Lord will honor your prudence and faithfulness. Take it from someone who knows!

Bev Dayton's Two Cents

Howard does the investing in our family, but he always tells me what he is thinking and asks for my advice. Real estate was his business, and I don't really understand a lot of the details. But I like the idea of not losing our home and other assets if something goes wrong with an investment.

That approach has kept us from some investments because either we did not have enough money or the lender was not willing for the investment to be the only security for the loan. That's always been fine with me. I'd rather not lose sleep and not have the stress of investment debt hanging over our heads.

TAKING STOCK

1. What are your investing and business goals?

2. Will you use debt to fund these goals? If so, describe your plan to pay it off.

3. Take some time to reflect honestly on your current financial situation, especially in light of what you've just read. Jot down the things that stood out most to you in this chapter.

4. Do you really believe the Lord is able to supply what you need to succeed financially? (Just let that question simmer for a while.)

There is one huge danger in consolidating
your loans . . . If you haven't solved
the problems that put you into
debt . . . you'll end up worse off.

CHAPTER SIXTEEN

Loan Consolidation and Home Equity Loans

im Connor e-mailed me again. His excitement was obvious. "Hi, Howard. My bank sent an application for a home equity loan. And it looks dynamite!

"We can consolidate all our credit card balances and car loans into one loan that has a much lower interest rate than we're paying now. And best of all, the interest will be tax deductible.

"What do you think? Should I go for it?" Boy, was I glad he asked. And I hope you ask before you move on that option. Before you take such a serious financial step, you need to understand how it all works and what it could mean for your financial future.

LOAN CONSOLIDATION: PROS AND CONS

The Pros of Consolidation

In theory, consolidating a number of higher-interest loans into one lower-interest loan makes a lot of sense. Consolidated loans typically offer lower monthly payments, and making just one payment is simpler.

If you have outstanding credit card balances, student loans, auto payments, and mortgages, you may be a candidate for loan consolidation. You have many options from which to choose: taking a personal loan from your bank or credit union, rolling your credit card balances to a low-rate card, or borrowing against the equity in your home.

But there are some downsides to consider as well.

The Big Downside of Consolidation

There is one huge danger in consolidating your loans, and I can't stress this enough. Here it is: If you haven't solved the problems that put you into debt in the first place, you'll end up worse off—and probably much worse off. You'll jump from the frying pan into the fire. You are just digging yourself into a deeper hole. Let me explain.

Surveys confirm that about two-thirds of those who borrow against their home equity to pay off credit cards run up more credit card debt within two years. They have not changed their habits.

If you cannot regularly spend less than you earn, you will continue racking up new debt. You will have to wrestle with not only the consolidation loan but also with the new debts you incur. So, as attractive as the idea is, I warn people not to consolidate because the false sense of relief often leads them into a deeper financial hole. At least wait until you have changed your spending habits and have a monthly surplus. Do yourself a favor: Hate debt; start paying it off; spend less than you earn. Then, if you still have a need, consider the option to consolidate your loans.

HOME EQUITY LOANS

How They Work

Home equity loans are simply additional mortgages. Banks and other mortgage lenders use the equity in your home as the collateral that secures the new loan. Home equity loans are one of the most popular types of debt-consolidation options available. And millions of consumers have gone down that road.

Borrowing against home equity was once tough to do and commonly understood as a bad idea. Times have really changed! Today, lenders encourage you to take this previously unthinkable risk.

There are two main ways to tap into your home equity: through a home equity loan (second mortgage) or a home equity line of credit.

Most lenders offer home equity loans that max out at 80 to 100 percent of the house's value, minus any already-existing mortgage. Suppose your home is worth $200,000 and you owe $100,000 on your mortgage. You would be eligible for a loan between $80,000 and $100,000 ($200,000 value minus $100,000 mortgage = $100,000 x 80% to 100%). The higher the loan-to-value, the higher the rate of interest you are going to pay.

Their Appeal

Home equity loans are attractive because lenders usually charge a lower interest rate and the repayment is spread over a longer period of time. That means that the monthly payment becomes smaller yet and cash is freed up for you to spend.

Tax-deductible interest is another big carrot lenders use to entice homeowners into using their home equity to fund major purchases and consolidate debt.

If you itemize your taxes, you can deduct the interest paid on home equity loans. However, there are limitations. Generally, you can deduct the interest on a maximum of $100,000 in home equity loans. But you cannot deduct the interest on any portion of home equity loans that exceed the fair market value of the home. It gets pretty complicated peeling back all the tax ramifications. I suggest you consult your tax advisor for guidance.

"YES, WE'D LIKE TO TALK TO YOU ABOUT A HOME EQUITY LOAN FOR OUR DAUGHTER'S PROM DRESS."

©Andy Robertson. Used by permission.

Before You Sign Up, Check It Out

Don't make the decision to secure a home equity loan without understanding the risks and costs. If you cannot pay a credit card bill, the issuer can take you to court and sue you for recovery. With a home equity loan, however, failure to pay could cost you your home.

Fees and closing costs on a home equity loan can range from nothing to thousands of dollars. If there are no closing costs, however, there is usually some sort of catch, such as a prepayment penalty or the requirement to maintain a minimum loan balance for a certain period of time. Be sure to ask the lender for a written disclosure of all fees before you sign on the dotted line. Whatever you decide, make certain your decision is based on solid and reliable information. Never pursue a home equity loan out of desperation or impulse.

If you already have a home equity loan, I recommend that you try to prepay something toward the loan principal *every* month to pay it off as soon as possible. You can use the same principles we applied to paying off your primary mortgage. A little bit consistently over time can add up to significant savings.

A HOME EQUITY LINE OF CREDIT

With a home equity line of credit (HELOC), the lender approves you for a loan up to a certain amount, allowing you to borrow up to your determined "credit limit." The limit is usually equal to or less than the amount of equity you have in your home.

Think of an HELOC as a giant credit card. You can borrow whenever you want and as much as you want—up to the credit limit. Your monthly payments are based on the amount you actually borrow. Like a credit card, an HELOC usually does not have to be paid off in a fixed number of months. But you are charged interest on any balance you maintain.

Several of the advantages of an HELOC are similar to a home equity loan: lower interest rates, tax-deductible interest, and lower closing costs than refinancing a mortgage.

But there are four major downsides to using HELOCs as well.

1. They can be a *huge* temptation. Just like a credit card, money is easily accessible and the tendency is to use it too often and impulsively rather than spending carefully. Soon you're back in debt way over your head.

2. Most of them carry variable interest rates that change as interest rates in the economy change. Make sure you can afford the higher payments that rising interest rates would require.

3. Lower interest rates and longer terms reduce the monthly payment. That is a good thing, right? Not if it actually *increases* the total amount of interest paid over the life of the loan. A lower rate paid over a longer time can end up costing considerably more. Some people who have financed their autos with HELOCs were still paying for the cars years after they no longer owned them!

4. HELOCs are interest-only loans. If one makes only the minimum payments, the balance never goes down.

SCAMS AND GIMMICKS

I want to offer you a gentle caution. There are some ill-intended people who prey on the financially desperate. If you don't take the time to understand all the facts, you could easily become the victim of a financial scam. Unfortunately, scam artists abound in the home equity loan business.

With that in mind, deal only with reputable lenders. No matter what, stay away from TV infomercials and spam e-mails promising you the deal of a lifetime to reduce your monthly payments even if you have bad credit. Checking with the Better Business Bureau is always a good idea. My best advice is to deal with someone you know and trust. If you are denied a loan by them, then it was likely for a very good reason. Better to stick with your current situation than to get further in debt.

DON'T FORGET TO PRAY

Using home equity to consolidate your loans and make major purchases always looks good on paper; that is why so many are doing it. How can you argue against lower monthly payments, tax-deductible interest, and no more credit card debt? But before you commit to using a home equity loan, take time to pray for the Lord's direction.

TAKING STOCK

Think about Proverbs 3:5–6: *"Trust in the LORD with all your heart, and lean not on your own understanding; in all your ways acknowledge him, and he will make your paths straight."*

You can easily "lean on your own understanding" when it comes to debt. Because debt is made so easily accessible you can easily fall for easy money options. I want you to develop the habit of seeking the Lord in every financial decision, especially when considering adding more debt.

Here's my personal paraphrase:

Before you pay, make sure you pray!

By cosigning, you promise to pay back the entire loan if the borrower does not. Please use sound judgment and *never* cosign a loan.

CHAPTER SEVENTEEN

Destitute of Mind: Watching Out for Cosigning

Hey, Howard!" I stopped feeding quarters into the parking meter and turned to see Tim Connor grinning broadly as he jogged toward me.

"I bet you've never seen anyone with so many questions," he said. "I wouldn't have bothered you with this one except that I just happened to see you here."

"No problem, Tim. What's up?"

"Well," he said, "Cindy and I both have an uneasy feeling about this, but we're caught in a bit of a dilemma—some family pressure. I was telling my brother-in-law, Mark Dixon, about how much you've helped us and the progress we're making—man, does he need the help—and he hit me with a request."

I could sense it coming . . .

"He can almost qualify for a loan—no interest for a year—on some furniture that's on sale. He's had some financial problems in the past and can do it only if I cosign for him. He says it won't cost me anything, and it will really help him out. I'd like to do it for him. In fact, I don't know how I would say no, but Cindy and I both feel a little uncomfortable. What do you think?"

"I think we need to get you and Cindy into a Crown small-group study," I answered, smiling. "In the meantime, let me tell you a quick story about someone else I know. Jack and Becky Kelly learned a very painful lesson that you can easily avoid. They handled their finances well, saving regularly for more than twenty years and building up a nest egg for retirement. They also had big, extremely generous hearts. So when a close friend asked them to cosign for a large loan to start a new business, they agreed. Unfortunately, they didn't understand the risk they were taking. The whole area of cosigning is loaded with hidden risks."

WHAT IS COSIGNING?

To understand what those risks are, I made sure Tim understood what cosigning is. You should too. Cosigning relates to debt. When a bank or lender does not feel an individual is a safe enough risk for credit, another person can cosign on the loan as a guarantor. *Anytime you cosign, you become legally responsible for the debt of another.* It is just as if you went to the bank, borrowed the money, and gave it to your friend or relative who is asking you to cosign.

In effect, by cosigning, *you* promise to pay back the entire loan if the borrower does not.

A Federal Trade Commission study found that 50 percent of those who cosigned for bank loans ended up making the payments. And 75 percent of those who cosigned for finance company loans ended up making the payments! Those are pretty good odds that if you cosign, you'll pay.

Few cosigners, however, plan for default. But the casualty rate is so high because the professional lender has analyzed the loan and told himself, *I won't touch this with a ten-foot pole unless I can get someone who is financially responsible to guarantee this loan.*

Proverbs 22:26–27 vividly describes what happened to Jack and Becky Kelly when their friend's business failed and the friend couldn't make the payments. *"Do not be among those who give pledges, among those who become guarantors for debts. If you have nothing with which to pay, why should he take your bed from under you?"* (NASB). That's precisely what happened to Jack and Becky. The lender sued the Kellys for the loan. They lost not only their retirement nest egg but also other personal property, including their bed!

Fortunately, Scripture gives us clear direction concerning cosigning. Proverbs 17:18 reads, *"It is poor judgment to co-sign a friend's note, to become responsible for a neighbor's debts"* (NLT). The phrase "poor judgment" is literally translated "destitute of mind"! God wants us to avoid making this sort of pledge, even though it can feel kindhearted and compassionate. The risk is too high. So please use sound judgment and *never* cosign a loan.

Cosigning for Children

Parents often cosign for their children's first automobile or some other form of credit. Bev and I decided not to do this. We wanted to model for our children the importance of not cosigning, and we wanted to discourage them from using debt (see chapter 20, "Teaching Kids About Debt").

Instead, we trained them to plan ahead and save for the purchase of their first car. And to encourage them, we tried to match what they were saving. It brought the family closer together and gave our children a sense of genuine accomplishment.

What to Do If You've Already Cosigned

If you have already cosigned for a loan, Scripture gives you advice. Proverbs 6:1–5 reads,

> *If you co-sign a loan for a friend or guarantee the debt of someone you hardly know—if you have trapped yourself by your agreement and are caught by what you said—quick, get out of it if you possibly can! You have placed yourself at your friend's mercy. Now swallow your pride; go and beg to have your name erased. Don't put it off. Do it now! Don't rest until you do. Save yourself like a deer escaping from a hunter, like a bird fleeing from a net.* (NLT)

Howard's paraphrase: *Do whatever it takes to get out, quickly! Beg if you have to.*

That's pretty urgent counsel, isn't it? But you can see how strongly the Lord feels about this type of high-risk debt. Don't even go there!

When I first learned this principle of not cosigning, it *was* too late. I'd already cosigned on a loan for a business partner. So I received permission from my partner to approach the bank and ask that I be relieved of this obligation. Then I showed the banker Proverbs 6:1–5 and explained why I was asking to be removed from the loan as a cosigner. The lender refused, but I had done my part in seeking to obey the principle. By God's grace, my partner ultimately paid off the loan.

Going Forward

Tim looked at me with an appreciative smile. "I really appreciate this, Howard. Not only have you confirmed why we were uncomfortable with the request, but that last story shows me how I can explain to my brother what he wouldn't otherwise understand. It's nothing personal, it's a biblical principle. By the way, how do I get into one of those Crown small-group studies?"

Bev's Two Cents

I never thought much about cosigning until a close family member asked Howard and me to cosign so he could purchase a modest home. He had managed his finances well but had spent all his savings dealing with a health problem.

We wanted to help, but we knew the Bible discouraged cosigning. We asked several other family members if they would join us in giving enough for the down payment. They agreed and that eliminated the need for anyone to cosign. This approach actually brought the family closer together, the Lord was honored, and our family member bought his home.

Well, that's the way it ought to work, don't you agree? Following God's roadmap, including avoiding the dangerous detour of cosigning, will eventually lead you to experience the blessings of true financial freedom.

TAKING STOCK

In Scripture God is speaking clearly and directly on this topic. There's no escaping this principle: Don't cosign for anyone, ever.

When God makes Himself so abundantly clear, how should we respond?

If you think of the Bible as the roadmap, this particular principle comes as a road sign warning of danger ahead. He is so good and loving, and He wants to protect you from a serious accident that could cause you long-term financial injury.

Take a few minutes to recommit yourself to staying on God's journey toward true financial freedom. Thank Him for the road signs found in the Bible that will guide you safely along the way.

Finance companies that deal primarily in debt-
consolidation loans charge enormous fees
and closing costs, [and are quick]
to turn the loan over to collections.

CHAPTER EIGHTEEN

Credit **to Avoid**

Tim called again for some advice. "A friend at work is having a really tough time financially," he explained. "He's been working at the company for only about six months. Turns out he lost his previous job and was out of work for almost a year. It destroyed his finances.

"He's been getting loans from finance companies—even some payday loans. I'm sure they're charging him an arm and a leg. He's going deeper and deeper in the hole. What should I tell him to do?"

Before he even finished the question, a melody floated through my mind. "Do you remember the old song Tennessee Ernie Ford used to sing?" I asked. "It goes something like this:

> You load sixteen tons, what do you get?
> Another day older and deeper in debt
> Saint Peter don't you call me 'cause I can't go
> I owe my soul to the company store."[1]

Tim laughed. "That must have been just a little before my time, but it sounds like it fits."

"Unfortunately, it does," I answered. "It's all about going backwards. The coal mining company provided food and housing at such high costs and interest rates that their workers were enslaved to the business. They could never earn enough to pay off the debt.

"Today, it's not the employer, it's some of the lenders that charge ridiculously high interest. They prey upon two kinds of people: those who don't know any better and those who have no other place to go because normal lenders consider them too high a risk. But even people who are high credit risks need to avoid those lenders like the plague! Once you get caught in their web, it seems impossible to get out."

FINANCE COMPANIES

Interest rates charged by finance companies are generally sky-high. The rates may run as high as prime rate *plus* 10 percent. People use these companies because their credit is not good enough to work with conventional lenders, and, in most cases, they are desperate for cash.

Finance companies that deal primarily in debt-consolidation loans charge enormous fees and closing costs. Pay attention to the difference between the interest rate offered and the annual percentage rate (APR). Closing costs on a conventional mortgage might increase the APR by half a percent. Any increase greater than that should send a clear signal: Stay away!

Another characteristic of finance companies is their lack of cooperation when payments are late. They are much quicker than conventional lenders to "pull the trigger" and turn the loan over to collections.

That means potentially serious damage to your credit score, and it could be years before you can recover. So make certain you understand what you're getting into.

PAYDAY LOANS

Payday loans, also known as "payroll advances" and "deferred deposits," are loans issued against a paycheck. These short-term loans usually range from $100 to $500 and represent a rapidly growing $1 billion-a-year industry. You see the storefront shops complete with neon signs popping up all over town these days. That's because the payday loan business is booming!

The Federal Trade Commission warns that the typical APR on payday loans is *391 percent*! Imagine borrowing $300 for two months and then owing $495. That's robbery! But it's happening all the time for people who need a quick way out of financial trouble.

Here's how they work. The borrower writes a postdated check for the amount of the loan plus a fee. The lender holds the check until the borrower receives his paycheck. Then the borrower takes cash to the lender or the lender deposits the postdated check. If the borrower cannot pay back the loan on time, it becomes horrendously expensive.

Payday loans are *predatory*—that means they're designed to keep borrowers in debt. Let me restate that in case you missed it. These lenders act intentionally to keep borrowers in bondage to debt. They make so much money they don't want anyone to escape. Amazingly, 91 percent of their business comes from people desperate enough to make five or more of these loans per year. But there are even more credit sources to avoid.

PAWNSHOP LOANS

Pawnshop loans are short-term loans secured by a piece of property or item of value that is sold if the loan is not paid on time. Interest rates range from 2 percent to 25 percent *per month,* depending on the laws of the state. Many people who utilize pawnshop loans never recover the property they pawned for cash. At times, people get in such desperate situations they end up pawning valuable property that they'll likely never see again.

If you're to the point where you're considering this option, then you need some real financial guidance.

AUTO TITLE LOANS

These loans are usually for thirty days and are secured by a car title. An individual can borrow cash based on the value of his or her car. The high interest rates are not the biggest downside of a title loan, however. If the borrower fails to make the loan payment on time, the lender can repossess the vehicle.

One consumer advocate said, "Car title loans are really legalized car theft because you lose the entire car equity no matter what the loan amount is."

TAX-REFUND LOANS

There is another type of quick-fix loan related to your tax refund. Millions of people look forward to April 15 each year because they are getting a tax refund and need the check from Uncle Sam. Some are so cash-strapped they can't wait for the IRS refund; they get a tax-refund loan instead.

Many tax preparers offer this service for a fee. What they neglect to tell their clients is that the interest rate they pay can run well into the triple figures on an annualized basis. You would think, *There oughta be a law!* Well, there is, but the major tax preparers have a way to avoid state usury laws designed to protect the public. They team up with banks chartered in states like Delaware and South Dakota that have no interest rate caps. Countless unsuspecting consumers have fallen prey to this trap. There really is a better way.

People can get quick refunds without the expense of this kind of loan. Fourteen days is the average turnaround time for electronic filers who provide the IRS with electronic deposit information for their bank account. It helps to stay ahead of the tax return schedule and file in advance of the tax return due date. That almost guarantees a quick turnaround on your tax refund check.

OTHER LENDERS TO AVOID

The Internal Revenue Service

There are two other potential lenders whom you may not recognize and need to avoid: the Internal Revenue Service and certain supplemental retirement plans. People who don't pay their taxes on time get whacked with penalties and interest from the IRS.

There are two things to remember when dealing with the Internal Revenue Service. First, even if you do not have the money to pay your tax bill, go ahead and file your return on time. Otherwise, you will be assessed the IRS's failure-to-file penalty of 5 percent per month (up to a maximum of 25 percent) of your tax bill.

Second, run *toward* the IRS and not *away* from them. Take the initiative to communicate. Despite the horror stories you may have heard, many of the agents are very helpful. Visit their Web site at www.irs.gov and click on "Taxpayer Advocate" if you need personalized assistance with a thorny issue.

Your 401(k) or 403(b)

Employers do not have to offer a loan feature with their 401(k) or 403(b) retirement plans, but 83 percent of workers covered by those plans can borrow against their accounts. And about 20 percent of them actually do it.

People who borrow from their retirement plan think it is a smart move because they are paying interest to themselves rather than to another lender.

That part is true, but there are hidden risks. Perhaps the greatest is that if they lose their job, they must repay the loan quickly, usually within weeks. If that is not possible, the loan balance is taxed as income, plus they have to cough up a 10 percent penalty for premature distribution. As if the loss of a job weren't bad enough!

Like home equity, the funds in retirement plans should be left alone to grow and provide for future needs.

GOING FORWARD

The temptation to fix your money woes with these types of quick-cash solutions can be very strong—especially if you're feeling a sense of desperation. But I urge you to consider the real costs involved in taking that path. The temporary relief will quickly fade when those high interest payments start piling up.

You'll never regret applying what God says about handling money. You can do it, I know you can, and God will help you every step of the way.

TAKING STOCK

Make this following commitment before you journey ahead:

> I promise never to give in to the temptation of quick financial fixes using these high interest-rate solutions. And for the good of my financial future I promise to avoid them to gain temporary relief.
>
> Name _____.
>
> Date _____.

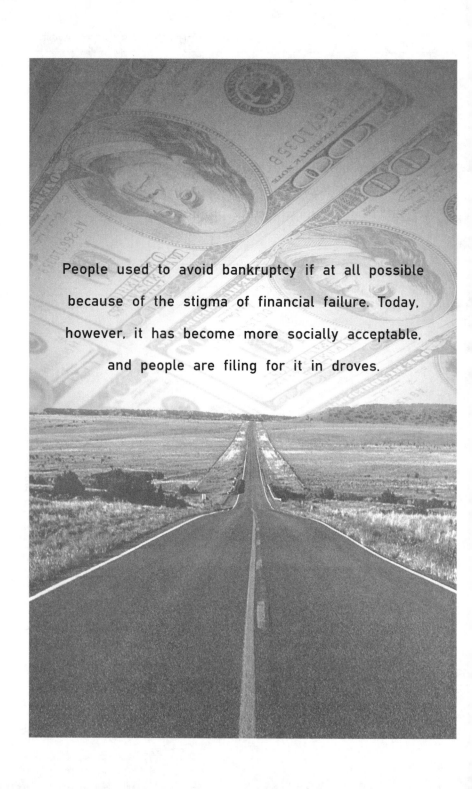

People used to avoid bankruptcy if at all possible because of the stigma of financial failure. Today, however, it has become more socially acceptable, and people are filing for it in droves.

Bankruptcy

Tim and Cindy were making great progress in spite of the short-term pain of really cutting back on their spending. The debt snowball was picking up speed, and credit card balances were shrinking quickly. During one of our meetings, Cindy raised a new issue.

"I was hoping I wouldn't need to talk about this," she started uncomfortably, "but it's not getting better, and I don't see how it can. I need some advice about my sister's situation."

"We'll try," I said, looking over at Bev. I had no idea what to expect. "What's the problem?"

Cindy took a deep breath, trying to keep her composure as she answered. "She called this morning and said that she had talked to an attorney about bankruptcy. I'm so worried for her. I know she's under a lot of stress, and it seems like this might really help her, but I just don't know what to think about it."

Bev leaned over and put her hand on Cindy's arm. Tim did

the same from the other side. "One thing is for sure," I said. "Your sister is fortunate to have people around her who care so much. Tell us about her situation—everything that led up to this."

"Well, her name is Rachel. She married her high school sweetheart while they were juniors in college. His name is Jack. They both grew up in middle-income homes and started their careers and family right after college. Like us, they thought they should be able to live the same lifestyle as our parents—without waiting for twenty years to build up to it. You know what that means: a ton of debt.

"But that was only the beginning. After their third child was born, Jack suddenly filed for divorce. It was a total shock, not only to us, but even to Rachel. She was devastated. And then to make matters even worse, he moved to another state and stopped the child support payments."

My heart sank. That wasn't the first time I had heard such a story. Jack left Rachel with three young children, no alimony or child support, a large home mortgage, a car loan, and more than $25,000 in credit card debt. She was completely unaware that Jack had racked up the credit card debt. And when the creditors started calling, she learned that *she* was responsible for this debt because the cards were also in her name.

Here was a young, single-parent mom earning a limited income with what felt like unlimited expenses. Bankruptcy was indeed staring her in the face.

AN ALARMING TREND

Rachel is not alone. Sadly, for all kinds of reasons, people are declaring bankruptcy in record numbers. This year there will be more than 1.5 million bankruptcies filed. To put that number into perspective, twenty years ago one out of every three hundred households went bankrupt. This year one out of every sixty-nine will go under. If this trend were to stop rising and remain constant at this year's number, it means that during the next ten years, *one of every seven households in the U.S. would declare bankruptcy.* Look at the graph.

U.S. BANKRUPTCY FILINGS
MILLIONS OF FILINGS

SOURCE: ABA WORLD MAGAZINE

People used to avoid bankruptcy if at all possible because of the stigma of financial failure. Today, however, it has become more socially acceptable, and people are filing for it in droves.

GOD'S PERSPECTIVE ON BANKRUPTCY

The Bible never prohibits bankruptcy, but it does discourage it. Psalm 37:21 reads, *"The wicked borrow and do not repay, but the righteous give generously."* We should make every effort to avoid bankruptcy. However, I believe bankruptcy to be permissible for the following reasons:

1. A creditor forces the borrower into bankruptcy.
2. The borrower experiences such extreme financial difficulties

that there is no option. This option needs to be exercised only after all others have been explored.

3. The emotional health of the borrower is at stake. If the debtor's emotional health is at stake because of inability to cope with the pressure of aggressive creditors, bankruptcy can be an option.

Here's an example of reason three. When Rachel's husband deserted the family, he left behind bills and debts that were more than Rachel could afford. The emotional trauma of the unwanted divorce, coupled with harassment from unsympathetic creditors, were too much for her to bear. She needed the emotional and financial relief bankruptcy provided.

THE DOWNSIDE OF BANKRUPTCY

Declaring bankruptcy should not be a cavalier decision. Among the consequences for those who resort to it are that (1) a bankruptcy remains on their credit report for *ten* years, and (2) it often impairs their ability to obtain future credit at reasonable interest rates. Potential employers and landlords are also likely to learn of a past bankruptcy. It can haunt people for some time, and although it provides relief, it is not exactly the fresh start that some advertise.

Bankruptcy is a relatively complicated legal procedure. Since it is a court-monitored activity, several people are involved including the bankruptcy judge, a trustee, and the person's creditors. Depending upon state law and the form of bankruptcy chosen, people may get to keep some or most of their assets. Some states, for example, allow people to keep their clothes and a car. Other states let them keep their home, car, and other assets. Bankruptcy stops most but not all garnishments, depending on the reason for the garnishment.

Most people are not able to discharge *all* of their debts through bankruptcy. They are still obligated to pay child support, alimony, most student loans, and taxes they owe. Consulting an experienced bankruptcy attorney will help you sort out all the issues.

TYPES OF BANKRUPTCY

There are three types of bankruptcy available. Chapter 11 is business bankruptcy, and you need to consult an attorney experienced in that area of law if you are contemplating it. Chapter 7 and Chapter 13 are the two types of personal bankruptcy.

Chapter 7 Bankruptcy

Chapter 7 is the more radical of the two personal bankruptcies. It provides for complete elimination of personal debt and is sometimes referred to as straight bankruptcy or total liquidation. Any possessions that the law does not specifically allow to be kept are sold, with the cash proceeds going to the creditors. The bankruptcy is then discharged, and creditors can no longer try to collect payments. Chapter 7 usually takes three to five months from the date of filing to the final discharge, and it can occur only once in any six-year period.

Chapter 13 Bankruptcy

Also known as debt adjustment, Chapter 13 involves a reorganization plan that enables people to make repayment according to their income. Foreclosures and collections are suspended while the repayment plan is drafted. A trustee appointed by the court receives a portion of the borrower's income and pays back all or part of the debt—usually over a three-to-five-year time frame.

In 2005, the U.S. Congress approved a new bankruptcy law that established a new test for measuring a debtor's ability to repay. If a borrower's income is above the state's median income, the bankruptcy judge can require a Chapter 13 repayment plan. The plan mandates repayment of at least $100 a month for five years to the creditors.

The law also requires people filing for bankruptcy to pay for credit counseling, and it restricts the homestead exemption to $125,000 in those states that allow debtors to keep their homes.

Top priority among creditors is given to a spouse's claim for child support, and there are special accommodations for active-duty service members, low-income veterans, and those with serious medical conditions. All in all, personal bankruptcy may be an option, but there are many issues you need to understand before proceeding.

Visit www.crownfreeandclear.org for links to more detailed information on bankruptcy.

WHAT IF YOU HAVE DECLARED BANKRUPTCY?

Repaying Your Debts

Bankruptcy can provide the opportunity for people to regain their financial stability. But here's something important to understand: If you've declared bankruptcy, don't carry a load of guilt. Learn what God wants to teach you from the difficult experience. And—are you ready for this—even if you are no longer *legally* obligated to repay the debts terminated through bankruptcy, you should seek to repay them. That's what God really desires.

Following through and repaying your debts will develop your character, and you will be a godly example to your creditors. Interestingly, some of the most successful people I know in business—and in life—have made the hard, right decision to repay debts extinguished by bankruptcy.

Seek counsel from a competent attorney to determine the

legal way to attempt repayment. For large debt, that may be a long-term goal largely dependent on God's supernatural provision of resources.

Understanding the 1099 Form

At the end of a bankruptcy, some people receive a form 1099 from creditors listing their discharged debt as income. However, debts discharged from bankruptcy do not count as income. As with other important documents, any related to a bankruptcy should be kept in case the facts are ever disputed.

THE IMPORTANCE OF LEGAL COUNSEL

People considering a bankruptcy should hire an honest, reputable attorney—one who is an experienced specialist in this area of the law. The benefit of hiring a Christian attorney is that he or she will honor biblical principles and provide spiritual encouragement as well.

TAKING STOCK

Don't underestimate how difficult bankruptcy can be. If you are considering it, I pray that you will use this time to draw especially close to God. Read the Bible daily and nurture your relationship with God. Jesus Christ cares for you and has promised, *"Never will I leave you; never will I forsake you"* (Hebrews 13:5).

When children become faithful with small amounts,
they are prepared to assume greater responsibility.
After they learn to handle quarters wisely,
they are ready for a few dollars.

CHAPTER TWENTY

Teaching Kids About Debt

T im and Cindy continued making progress and they were understandably grateful. But our next meeting revealed a new concern that was bothering them. "Our son, Matt, and daughter, Jennifer, are terrific kids . . ." explained Tim.

"But we've done nothing to train them about the dangers of debt," Cindy interrupted. "Most of their lives they've seen two parents abuse debt. What can we do?"

I had met their children during an earlier visit to the Connors's home. "Remind me," I asked. "How old are they?"

"Matt is eight and Jennifer is six," Cindy responded.

I smiled. "I am so excited to hear that you're thinking about that now. Most parents just take that part of their children's education for granted. But it's something for which the parents must take responsibility. Proverbs 22:6 tells us, *'Train a child in the way he should go, and when he is old he will not turn from it.'* You are starting at a great time!"

SEEING THE BIG PICTURE

The fundamental strategy for training children to handle money is the *Little-Big* principle found in Luke 16:10: *"He who is faithful in a very little thing is faithful also in much"* (NASB).

When children become faithful with small amounts, they are prepared to assume greater responsibility. After they learn to handle nickels, dimes, and quarters wisely, they are ready for a few dollars. When they manage a few dollars well, they are prepared for handling more.

Parents should be as systematic in equipping children to handle money as teachers are in teaching them to write. Children first learn the alphabet and then how to spell "cat." Each year they learn more complex words and grammar. Eventually, they are able to write term papers and write e-mails and letters. Learning is a process that happens in stages.

GRADUATING TO GREATER RESPONSIBILITY

The goal is to steadily increase responsibility so that eventually your children are independently managing all their finances—with the exception of food and shelter—by their senior year in high school. That way, parents are available to advise their children as they make financial decisions while still at home, but turn more and more responsibility over to them.

Unfortunately, the majority of children graduate from high school totally ill equipped to handle money. One college student I know admitted how shocked he was to learn that credit card purchases actually had to be paid for later! That surprise paled in comparison to the shock his parents received when his credit card statement arrived with an outstanding balance of $11,350!

By the time your children are in their junior year of high

school, they should open a checking account and get a secured credit card. Parents can then show them how to reconcile their checkbook each month, coaching them to use the credit card wisely and pay it off in full and on time every month. Once those disciplines are in place they will likely stay in place for a lifetime.

PARENTS AS MVPS

Parents should be *MVP Parents*. MVP is an acronym that describes the three methods to teach children God's way of handling money: Modeling, Verbal communication, and Practical opportunities. All three elements are needed to train your children in the area of finances. Let's take a closer look at each method.

1. Modeling

Since children soak up parental attitudes toward money like a sponge soaks up water, parents must model God's principles of handling money. Paul recognized the importance of modeling when he said, *"Follow my example, as I follow the example of Christ"* (1 Corinthians 11:1). Nothing influences children more than watching their parents live out what they believe. That's especially true in the area of finances. Your kids watch how you spend money, pick up on your attitudes toward buying on credit, and see your patterns of spending and saving. Make certain what you say about money is consistent with what you do. Your children are listening *and* watching you.

2. Verbal Communication

We should verbally instruct our children in the ways of the Lord. The Lord said to His people, *"These commandments that I give you today are to be upon your hearts. Impress them on your children. Talk about them when you sit at home and when you walk along the road, when you lie down and when you get up"* (Deuteronomy 6:6–7).

Consistently tell your children how the practical truths from the Bible apply to their finances. Use natural times, such as when you're grocery shopping or walking through the hardware store or waiting in line at the bank drive-up—these are perfect opportunities to instruct your children on the wise use of money. As they mature, help them understand that these principles are a gift from a loving God who wants them to handle money wisely. That attitude will be a great blessing for the rest of their lives.

3. Practical Opportunities

Give your children opportunities to apply what they have heard and seen. Design these experiences to be appropriate for their age and unique personality. Young children, for example, are not yet able to grasp abstract concepts, so their practical experiences need to be tangible and easy to understand.

When our children were young, I drew a graphic illustration of our debt. As we paid down the principal each month, they used crayons to fill in our progress toward becoming debt-free. That "hands-on" experience gave them a sense of how long it takes to get out of debt, providing us with many opportunities to communicate our commitment to becoming totally free and clear of debt.

One father I know loaned his son and daughter the money to buy bicycles. He drew up a credit agreement with a repayment schedule that included the interest charged. After the children completed the long process of paying off the loans, the family celebrated with a "mortgage burning" picnic at the beach. The father told me his children appreciated those bikes more than anything else they had and vowed to avoid debt in the future.

PARENTS BECOME COACHES

As children leave home to marry or pursue their own careers, your role as parents changes. Once adults, children no longer remain under your authority. Parents should assume the role of coach, mentor, and encourager. Adult children will naturally resist too much parental involvement and look rather for encouragement and support.

Bev and I have thoroughly enjoyed this relationship with our adult children and their spouses. I believe parents earn this role by expressing their love and care to their children and their spouses in thoughtful and appropriate ways. Bev has been faithful to *"train the younger women to love their husbands and children, to be self-controlled and pure, to be busy at home, to be kind, and to be subject to their husbands, so that no one will malign the word of God"* (Titus 2:4–5). In return, our daughter and daughter-in-law phone Bev almost every day asking for advice or just because they enjoy talking with her.

We have continued to encourage them to become free and clear of debt. We have offered, as long as we are able, to match a portion of any prepayment they make on their home mortgages. They and their spouses have made real progress toward getting their mortgages paid off and have appreciated this tangible expression of our love for them.

GRANDPARENTS ARE SPECIAL

Grandparents have a unique opportunity to influence their grandchildren, both when they're young and as adults. It is important for grandparents to play a *complementary* role in which they affirm the objectives of the parents. Too often parents and grandparents have not agreed on how to train the youngest generation, and this can lead to bruised relationships and ineffective training. Together they should discuss how the grandparents can participate most effectively.

Handling money God's way is one of the most practical legacies you can leave your children and grandchildren. Make sure your life is characterized by generosity, spending within your means, saving consistently, and staying out of debt. Modeling, communicating verbally, and offering real life opportunities will form within your children the discipline and character they need to live wisely and faithfully before the Lord.

TAKING STOCK

Training your children is an important spiritual priority. Showing them how to honor the Lord financially is critical to forge within them godly character, a vibrant faith, and a lifelong commitment to wise money management and to supporting God's work.

But you don't have to do it alone. There are many excellent resources for you and your family. I urge you to pursue the practical and creative help you need in order to teach these important principles to the next generation. Listed below are some resources my wife, Bev, and I have had the privilege of preparing for you and your children.

The ABCs of Handling Money God's Way, by Howard and Bev Dayton, Moody Publishers (for children ages 4–7).

The Secret of Handling Money God's Way, by Howard and Bev Dayton, Moody Publishers (for children ages 8–12).

The Teen Study, by Howard and Bev Dayton, Crown Financial Ministries.

Check out www.crown.org for additional help and resources.

I had everything I thought would give me happiness and a sense of accomplishment. However, I was experiencing neither happiness nor a sense of accomplishment.

CHAPTER TWENTY-ONE

A Debt You Cannot Pay

The last words Jesus spoke before dying on the cross were, *"It is finished!"* (John 19:30). These words are literally translated "paid in full." Jesus Christ paid a debt for us that we could never pay.

I was twenty-eight years old when I started attending a weekly breakfast with several young businessmen. It wasn't long before I was impressed by their energy and creative business savvy. But more than that, I was attracted to the quality of their lives. I didn't know what they had, but whatever it was, I wanted it.

SOMETHING IS MISSING

I was part owner of a successful restaurant and had married my wonderful wife. Together we lived in a comfortable home. I had everything I thought would give me happiness and a sense of accomplishment. However, I was experiencing neither happiness nor a sense of accomplishment. I knew something was missing.

The men with whom I met regularly spoke openly of their faith in God. I grew up going to church, but the religion I saw modeled for me as a youngster meant nothing to me as an adult. A friend described how I could enter into a personal relationship with Jesus Christ, explaining five truths from the Bible I had never understood before.

FIVE GREAT TRUTHS

Those five truths, which remain valid today, follow.

1. God loves you. He wants you to know Him and experience a meaningful life.

God desires an intimate relationship with each of us. The Bible teaches that *"God so loved the world that he gave his one and only Son, that whoever believes in him shall not perish but have eternal life"* (John 3:16). Also, Jesus said, *"I came that they may have life, and have it abundantly"* (John 10:10 NASB).

Derek Redmond had dreamed all his life of winning the Olympic gold medal in the 400-meter race. In the 1992 Olympics in Barcelona, Spain, he had that chance, running for his homeland, Great Britain. When the gun sounded for the semifinals, Derek knew that he had just started the race of his life.

He entered the backstretch at full speed, when suddenly a searing pain shot up his right leg. A torn hamstring sent Redmond sprawling onto the hard track.

Instinctively, Derek struggled to get up. Then, with the pain pounding, he began hopping on his one good leg toward the finish line. He might not win, but he would finish.

Suddenly, a large man came bounding from the stands. Pushing aside the startled security guards, he crossed onto the track and threw his arms around Derek. It was Jim Redmond, Derek's father.

"Son, you don't have to do this," he said.

"Yes, Dad, I do," Derek assured him.

"All right then, let's finish this thing together," said the older man. With the son's head frequently buried in his father's shoulder, as Derek's body shuddered with pain, the young British runner, helped by his father, crossed the finish line. The watching crowd rose to its feet, weeping and cheering.[1]

Derek Redmond did not win the gold medal that day. But he won something far more valuable. He walked away from the race with the memory of a father who not only cheered in the stands but also loved him too much to watch him suffer from a distance—a father who came down out of the stands and entered the race, staying with his son every step of the way.

You too have a heavenly Father who watches your life with eyes of love and affection. He cared for you too deeply to stay in heaven, looking down on you, watching you struggle. Instead, He came down in the person of His precious Son, Jesus Christ, to carry you all the way home. And He is committed to staying in this race with you until you too cross safely past the finish line.

2. We are separated from God.

God is holy—which means God is perfect and without sin, and He cannot have a relationship with anyone who is not perfect. My friend asked if I had ever sinned—done anything that would disqualify me from perfection.

"Many times," I admitted.

He explained that every person has sinned, and that the consequence of sin is separation from God. *"For all have sinned and fall short of the glory of God,"* the Scripture says. *"Your sins have cut you off from God"* (Romans 3:23; Isaiah 59:2 NLT).

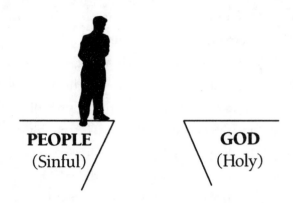

PEOPLE
(Sinful)

GOD
(Holy)

An enormous gap separates us from God. Individuals try without success to bridge this gap through their own efforts. Nothing—not education, wealth, wisdom, or power—can bridge the gap between us and God.

3. God's only provision to bridge this gap is Jesus Christ.

Jesus Christ died on the cross to pay the debt for your sin. Colossians 2:13–14 says it this way: *"[God] made you alive together with [Christ], having forgiven us all our transgressions, having cancelled out the certificate of debt . . . having nailed it to the cross"* (NASB).

Christ bridged the gap between God and people. Jesus said, *"I am the way and the truth and the life. No one comes to the Father except through me"* (John 14:6). *"But God demonstrates his own love for us in this: While we were still sinners, Christ died for us"* (Romans 5:8). Someone once wrote: "We had a debt we could not pay; Jesus paid the debt that He did not owe."

This diagram illustrates our union with God through Jesus Christ:

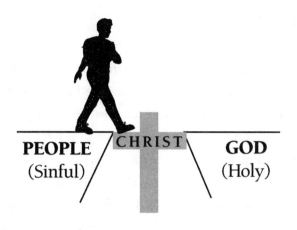

PEOPLE /CHRIST\ **GOD**
(Sinful) / \ (Holy)

4. This relationship is a gift from God.

My friend explained that by an act of faith I could receive the free gift of a relationship with God. The transaction appeared totally inequitable. I had learned in business that any time two people were convinced they were getting more than they were giving up, you had a transaction. But now I was being offered a relationship with God, and it was a free *gift*! *"For it is by grace you have been saved, through faith—and this not from yourselves, it is the gift of God—not by works, so that no one can boast"* (Ephesians 2:8-9).

5. We must each receive Jesus Christ individually.

I had only to ask Jesus Christ to come into my life to be my Savior and Lord. So I did! As my friends will tell you, I am a very practical person—if something does not work, I stop doing it quickly. I can tell you from more than thirty years of experience that a relationship with the living God works. And it is available to you through Jesus Christ. Nothing in life compares with the privilege of knowing Christ personally. We can experience true peace, joy, and hope when we know Him. We can be free and clear from the debt of sin we owe.

TAKING STOCK

If you desire to know the Lord and are not certain whether you have this relationship, I encourage you to receive Jesus Christ right now. Pray a prayer similar to this suggested one: "Father God, I need You. I'm sorry for my sin. I invite Jesus to come into my life as my Savior and Lord and to make me the person You want me to be. Thank You for forgiving my sins and giving me the gift of eternal life. Amen."

You might become totally debt-free, but without a relationship with Christ, it won't have any lasting value. If you asked Christ into your life, then you are free indeed! You have made the most important decision anyone could ever make.

I urge you to find a local church where you can begin to learn what it means to follow Jesus and to be encouraged by other Christians. Contact us at www.crownfreeandclear.org for more information on what it means to grow in your new relationship with Christ.

The road from debt to freedom from debt sometimes gets bumpy. But do not become discouraged and give up.

CHAPTER TWENTY-TWO

Free **and Clear!**

Bev and I were invited to attend a very special celebration.
Tim and Cindy Connor stood, holding hands. They
choked back tears as they looked around the room at
friends and family. "It's hard to believe," Tim said, "but
twelve years ago, Cindy and I were lost in the wilderness of debt. We'd
made a lot of poor financial decisions, and it was threatening our
marriage."

Cindy added, "We've invited you here to celebrate with us the
paying off of our last debt—our home mortgage. We hope this will
encourage some of you to do the same thing.

"As many of you know, it wasn't easy for us to get out of debt.
There were lots of challenges along the way. But we decided that we
weren't going to give up. And today we know how good it feels to
finally be free and clear from the bondage of debt."

THE JOURNEY IS WORTH THE EFFORT

The road from debt to freedom from debt sometimes gets bumpy; there are times when you will find yourself pulling off the road to regain your bearings or make some adjustments to your plan. At other times you will be slowed by an unexpected detour (expense) or an occasional wrong turn. All of that is expected on the journey. But do not become discouraged and give up. The destination of becoming free and clear from debt is worth the effort.

On New Year's Day of 1929, Georgia Tech played the University of California in the Rose Bowl. A California player named Roy Riegels recovered a fumble. Somehow he became confused and sprinted sixty-five yards—in the wrong direction! One of his teammates tackled him just before he crossed the opposing team's goal line. His mistake was made in full view of 80,000 screaming fans!

When the players filed off the field and went into their dressing rooms for halftime, Roy Riegels put a towel over his head, sat in a corner, and wept uncontrollably. The shame was unbearable.

When the timekeeper came in and announced that there were three minutes before the start of the second half, California coach Nibbs Price went over to Riegels and told him that he wanted him to start the second half.

Riegels looked up with tear-filled eyes and a bewildered expression. "Coach," he said, "I can't do it. I've disgraced you. I've disgraced the University of California. I've disgraced myself."

Coach Price put his hand on Riegels's shoulder and spoke these remarkable words: "Roy, the game is only half over. Your teammates need you now like they've never needed you before."

Roy went back in and played the second half. And those Georgia Tech players will tell you that they had never seen a man play football like Roy Riegels played during the second half of the game.

He was courageous, focused, and he never gave up. All he needed to finish well was a word of encouragement and the right perspective.[1]

Finishing your journey to become debt-free does not mean finishing without making mistakes. But it does mean learning from your mistakes, getting back on the road, and pursuing and setting your sights on the final destination: true financial freedom.

The apostle Paul said it this way: *"One thing I do: forgetting what lies behind and reaching forward to what lies ahead, I press on toward the goal for the prize of the upward call of God in Christ Jesus"* (Philippians 3:13–14 NASB).

Winston Churchill, Great Britain's prime minister during World War II, was invited to give the commencement speech at one of England's most prestigious college preparatory schools.

Churchill was a superb communicator, widely known for long and powerful speeches. When it came time for his address, he stood at the podium for a few moments in silence, gazing penetratingly into the eyes of the young students. Finally, his voice boomed, "Never give up! Never, ever give up! Never, ever, ever give up!" And he sat down. That was it. That's all he said, but the message was powerful.

I pray that this book has given you more appreciation for how much God loves and cares for you—and more appreciation for the Bible as a practical book filled with the truth and wisdom of God.

I hope you have grasped the vision of becoming debt-free and that you will "never, ever, ever give up" until you have achieved that goal.

TIM AND CINDY ARRIVE

As we pulled out of the Connors' driveway, Bev leaned over to me and said, "I couldn't help but think back to the first time we met Tim and Cindy. What a change! All I could think about were these words to describe them: from bondage and stress to freedom and peace." They made it. And you can too.

Notes

Chapter 18: Credit to Avoid

1. The song ""Sixteen Tons" was written by country singer Merle Travis in 1946. The chorus is based on a letter Travis received from his brother, John Travis, who wrote of journalist Ernie Pyle's death during World War II: "It's like working in the coal mines. You load sixteen tons and what do you get? Another day older and deeper in debt." This referred to the cash advances that miners could get for food and supplies from company-owned stores prior to paydays and the debt that ensued. Ford's recording sold two million copies in just two months, a record for a single title. For more information, see www.ernieford.com/Sixteen%20Tons.htm.

Chapter 21: A Debt You Cannot Pay

1. Claire Cloninger, *Dear Abba* (Dallas: Word, 1997), 15–16.

Chapter 22: Free and Clear!

1. Haddon Robinson, "The God of the Second Chance," *30 Good Minutes,* 2 February 1996, WTTW/TV, Chicago and VISN-TV; http://www. 30goodminutes.org/csec/sermon/robinson_4017.htm.

CROWN FINANCIAL MINISTRIES
True Financial Freedom

OUR VISION

Crown Financial Ministries' vision is to see followers of Christ in every nation faithfully living by God's financial principles in every area of their lives.

OUR MISSION

Our primary mission is to equip people worldwide to learn, apply, and teach God's financial principles so they may know Christ more intimately, be free to serve Him, and help fund the Great Commission.

OUR CORE VALUES

Crown strives to be Christ-centered, Word-based, Prayer-driven, Relationship-designed, People-taught, Servant-led, Excellence-developed, and Generations-intended in our thoughts and actions.

OUR MAJOR OBJECTIVE

Our major objective is to teach God's financial principles to 300 million people by September 15, 2015.

To learn more about Crown Financial Ministries and to obtain materials that help teach God's financial principles in your church or community, visit us online at <u>Crown.org</u> or call 1-800-722-1976.

Crown Financial Ministries
MONEY MAP
Your Visual Guide to True Financial Freedom

TRUE FINANCIAL FREEDOM

HOWARD DAYTON
WITH
CHUCK BENTLEY

ISBN# 1-56427-174-9

You may have noticed that *Free &
Clear* is a Destination 2 resource
on the *Crown Financial Ministries®
Money Map.*™

With over 100,000 units
distributed in its first printing,
the *Crown Money Map*™ is a
visual guide to true financial
freedom that shows 7 Destinations
to becoming financially free.

This step-by-step, full-color trip
of a lifetime has a fun and simple
layout, and you will be encouraged as you take each step along
this important journey.

To begin your journey now,
contact your local Christian
retailer or visit Crown online
at **Crown.org/MoneyMap**!

PC Software Budgeting Solution

Money Matters budgeting software is designed to help ease your financial burdens by doing a lot of the thinking for you. It keeps track of dates, budgets, and other details. Print checks, make deposits, track your portfolio. And biblical advice is always only one click away!

Some *Money Matters* 2007 software features include:

● The *Budgeting Assistant* walks you through the entire budgeting process.

● New reports give you even more detailed information about your *financial plan*, and they can be customized to fit your needs.

● The *Wisdom Portal* includes a huge database of financial advice, articles, and frequently asked questions to help you make wiser decisions.

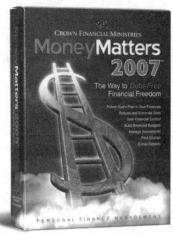

ISBN# 1-56427-049-1

To order, contact your local Christian retailer or visit Crown Financial Ministries at Crown.org.

Online Budgeting Solution

Crown™ Mvelopes® Personal is a Web-based home budgeting system that helps you save time and money while creating a long-term spending and savings plan.

● Easily create a household budget accessible from anywhere 24/7.

● Automatically retrieves your checking, savings, and credit card transactions—no typing in financial data!

● Optional online bill paying feature.

● Always know how much you have left to spend in each budget category.

● Most important, be content knowing that you have a smart saving and spending plan for you and your family.

Go to Crown.Mvelopes.com to view the Quick Tour and sign up for a FREE Trial Membership.

The Cash Organizer™ envelope budgeting system will simplify your budgeting plan by keeping you in control of your cash spending. It will hold you accountable by budget category – if there's no money left in a particular envelope, you're finished spending in that category until payday!

Bilingual
English-Spanish Edition
ISBN# 1-56427-059-9

Twelve tear-resistant envelopes keep each category neatly organized in a durable navy blue expanding file. *The Cash Organizer*™ also comes with preprinted category stickers, a handy ledger booklet for recording your transactions, and a practical teaching pamphlet on managing your money according to biblical principles.

With the *Bill Organizer*, there's no more searching frantically for that misplaced phone bill or wondering if the power bill has been paid! This expanding file of durable blue plastic contains 12 tabbed pockets that can be customized easily to organize your bills by either category or due date! Preprinted stickers, ledger sheets for tracking your payments, and online bill reminder cards are included.

ISBN# 1-56427-041-6

To order, contact your local Christian retailer or visit Crown Financial Ministries at Crown.org.

These Bible-based resources use interesting stories and fun activities to teach kids the basics about money. Teach your children what the Bible says about money today and secure their financial futures tomorrow!

The ABC's of Handling Money God's Way

Student Workbook: ISBN# 0-8024-3152-6
Teacher's Guide: ISBN# 0-8024-3152-8

The Secret of Handling Money God's Way

Student Workbook: ISBN# 0-8024-3154-2
Teacher's Guide: ISBN# 0-8024-3153-4